DAVID MITCHELL was born in 1940 in Wellington, where he attended teachers college. Returning home after a formative European trip in the early 1960s, Mitchell became an active reader and promoter of his own and others' poetry. His collection *Pipe Dreams in Ponsonby* was published in 1972. Mitchell was awarded the Katherine Mansfield Fellowship in 1975 and in 1980 he toured nationally with Alan Brunton and Ian Wedde. He started and ran Poetry Live! in Auckland for three years from 1980. Despite a decline in health from the mid-1980s, Mitchell has continued to write and perform and completed, in 2002, a Bachelor of Arts from Victoria University in Wellington. He lives in Sydney.

MARTIN EDMOND is the author of the award-winning *Chronicle of the Unsung* (2004), *Waimarino County* (2007), *Luca Antara* (2006) and most recently *Zone of the Marvellous* (2009), for which he received a CLL Writers' Award.

NIGEL ROBERTS was born in New Zealand and has lived in Sydney since 1965. He has published three collections of poetry, *In Casablanca for the Waters* (1978), *Steps for Astaire* (1984) and *Déjà vu Tours* (1995). His selected poems will be published in 2011.

Steal Away Boy

selected poems of david mitchell

edited by Martin Edmond & Nigel Roberts

AUCKLAND UNIVERSITY PRESS

for Belinda, Sara, Genevieve

First published 2010

Auckland University Press
University of Auckland
Private Bag 92019
Auckland 1142
New Zealand
www.auckland.ac.nz/aup

Poems © David Mitchell
Selection and introduction © the editors, 2010

ISBN 978 1 86940 459 8

Publication is kindly assisted by

National Library of New Zealand Cataloguing-in-Publication Data
Mitchell, David, 1940-
Steal away boy : selected poems of David Mitchell /
edited by Martin Edmond and Nigel Roberts.
Includes index.
ISBN 978-1-86940-459-8
I. Edmond, Martin. II. Roberts, Nigel S. III. Title.
NZ821.2—dc 22

Facing page 1: Dave Mitchell, Balmain, 1973. Photograph by Ric Harris
Front cover: Dave Mitchell performing, Christchurch, 1973. Photograph by Keith
Nicolson, 28 Winchester Street, Port Lyttelton, Canterbury 8082, New Zealand,
www.photographer.co.nz
Back cover: Elsebeth and Dave, Kings Cross, 1965. Photograph by Albert
Cover design: Keely O'Shannessy

Printed by Printlink Ltd, Wellington

Contents

Five : Myths of Woolloomooloo

Six : Dark Fire

Introduction

I N THE PRE-DAWN OF 19 MARCH 2006, David Mitchell did a runner from the Alexandra Rest Home in Newtown, Wellington, where he had been housed for the previous year. It was no itinerant's flit, nor spur-of-the-moment thing. He was in trouble and he knew it. He needed help. His body systems were breaking down. He dressed in the dark and slipped out to a taxi waiting in Rintoul Street. He had with him his passport and an airline ticket bought with money scrimped from his invalid's pension. The driver popped the boot and placed therein a portable typewriter, a back-pack and a well travelled suitcase containing clothes, letters, papers, cricketing memorabilia and all the manuscripts that he possessed, both the originals and the photocopies bound into thick blue volumes. He left behind the usual detritus—and the bronze Katherine Mansfield Fellow medal he had been awarded in 1975. The taxi took him to the airport at Rongotai, where he boarded the early flight for Sydney. His daughter Sara lived there. He had phoned ahead and she would be at the other end to meet him. It was the latest, perhaps the last, of many flights to Australia. Steal away, boy . . .

HIS PARENTS CAME FROM ELSEWHERE. His father, David Eric Mitchell, was born into an Irish Jewish family in western Sydney in 1880; he was not partial to school and ran away to sea aged twelve; when he couldn't get a ship, he went rabbiting in the outback. In World War I he was a stoker on troop carriers and then a deckhand in the trans-Tasman trade; in 1923 he was paid off and put ashore at Napier after a cargo sling tore and dropped a length of rail iron that crushed his foot. Mitchell's mother, Rossetta Cousins, born 1903 in Strathclyde, was the fourth of nine children who,

Etta & Dave at Donald Street.
Courtesy Mitchell family

following two of her sisters, registered with the New Zealand immigration agency in Glasgow and in 1925 came out on the SS *Ruapehu*, to be employed as a domestic at Maraekakaho Station west of Hastings—and it was there, in the fiefdom of station owner Sir Douglas McLean, that this former stoker and domestic servant met.

They could not marry because Dave had contracted a previous liaison in Sydney; gossip drove them to Napier, and thence to Wellington. A premature child died along the way. Four more children—Ross (1929), Ann (1934), David (1940) and Stewart (1942)—were born at the Salvation Army's Bethany maternity home in Te Aro. In the capital Dave and Etta tended and lived aboard a coal hulk moored in the harbour: *I remember,* said Ross, *the floating dock coming in and whenever Dad rowed ashore, taking me in his little dinghy . . . him pointing out the big ships and where they came from.* In 1935 the family moved to Horopito in the King Country to run a boarding house for mill workers: *We would hitch a ride to Raetihi on a goods train and come home the same way . . . Mum came in contact with the Baptist Church . . . and the four of us would attend three services each Sunday.*

The Mitchells returned to Wellington in 1937 and lived at 61 Donald Street, Karori, for the next eleven years. It was a six-room house, a former manse, with a workshop underneath, from which issued handyman knick-knacks, furniture repairs and the neighbours' wooden toilet seats. Dave made the children toys that Etta painted. They worked at either end of a cross-cut saw, breaking down the fallen trees for firewood. There was a large hand-dug vegetable garden: it is tempting to read a family photograph of a Harvest Festival cornucopia, displayed at the Baptist Church hall under the legend *The Lord Has Visited His People In Giving Them Bread,* as a precognition of 'The Singing Bread'. In September 1939

Ruth 1:6. Courtesy Mitchell family

war broke out in Europe; four months later, on 10 January, David was born: from this point on familiars referred to his father as Old Dave.

During the war years the Mitchells took in boarders who, apart from one 'conchie', were cadets in government departments. Three of these were to die fighting in the Middle East; another went down with the RMS *Rangitane*. There are traces of war trauma in some of Mitchell's early poems, as well as glimpses of his father drilling, marching and policing the blackouts as a participant in the Emergency Precautions Scheme. After the war Old Dave helped build the municipal baths behind Karori school. When that finished he went on the benefit or found work cutting gorse on the Wellington hills. Later he was a lift attendant in the AMP Building at which time, every payday, he would bring home for the family a slab of fruit-cake from Adams Bruce.

Dad was Dad, said Ann. *He never lifted a finger to any of us. He would roar and swear and get out of the house down to his workshop in the basement when trouble brewed . . . Mum ruled the roost and did smack us. David remembers the belt which she would wave about chasing the boys and sometimes catch them and threaten to use the buckle end.* But Etta was also

quick to front up to anyone she felt had wronged her kids: a short, fiesty, determined woman almost as wide as she was tall.

The 1947 polio epidemic closed all schools for five months. Lessons were broadcast and thus the family acquired its first radio. 1947 was also the year of the single edition of the *Donald Street Post*, which David Mitchell, sole author and publisher, sold to his parents and siblings for a penny a copy. He also wrote *stories which I later collected into a thick volume, entitled* Cowboy and Pirate Stories *(1951)*; and a saga, *Flying Saucers Have Landed*, that was serialised on the classroom wall at Karori primary school.

When, the following year, Old Dave collapsed, haemorrhaging from a peptic ulcer, the family, under pressure, moved to a state house in Aro Street. Dave was not expected to live. The older kids had to step up: Ann took over household duties. Ross went sea-gulling on the wharves and supervised the education of his two younger brothers; he remembers buying David many volumes of adventure yarns from Whitcombe & Tombs. Against expectations, Old Dave recovered and normal life resumed.

They made their own entertainment. *We used to sing Scottish pop songs of the day*, Ann said, *sitting around the fire in the evenings and Mum would recite Burns and Scott poems. Dad sang too—Australian bush songs—and we'd all join in. Mum was very nervous performing in public but once sang in Karori church; she knew all the words by heart and got great applause.* In Sydney Old Dave had been in the Salvation Army band and would play hymns ('Abide with Me', 'Lead Kindly Light') on mouth organ and trumpet.

Mitchell recalled *poems . . . amongst the stories & illustrations in the books that lay about that old wooden house in Karori ; and later too, in Aro Street—I remember Lord Randall, and other scottish ballads . . . It was not until the fifties that I consciously set my hand to emulating the old 'makars'. A secondary influence was my mother who . . . pestered me with requests for vocabulary for her crosswords . . . Henry Lawson, Banjo Paterson & Benjamin Disraeli were my father's favourite authors.*

The Mitchells at Donald Street. Courtesy Mitchell family

OLD DAVE DIED OF PNEUMONIA IN 1953; chaos ensued. Because the couple had never married, Etta was not entitled to a Widow's Pension and so had to work full time to earn the family's keep; first as a bathroom attendant at the DIC (Drapery Importing Company), a department store in Lambton Quay; later, and for the rest of her working life, as a records clerk for the Army. In that same year David went to Wellington College: *five or six years of adolescent anguish commencing in 1953 incl 6 months with one leg in plaster from ankle to hip and learning to cope with bullies on all fronts, or so it seemed, at home, at school, at church and in the world at large.*

He was a good athlete and loved sport: cricket, rugby, fives, swimming, diving, and water-polo, which he played at the Karori and Thorndon baths. In cricket he was an all-rounder and in rugby a second five-eighth. He made all the teams and in the photographs looks sartorially elegant, confident, handsome and by these qualities set apart from his fellows. At some time in the early 1950s the New Zealand captain, all-rounder John Reid, anointed Mitchell as one of Wellington's five outstanding schoolboy cricketers; and in the fifth form at Wellington College his rugby coach was Sam Meads, cousin of Colin and Stan. Mitchell wrote in a letter, *Wellington gets that hazy smoky look in the mornings now & I know its time for rugby. I can feel it, its like the flu coming on. I love rugby, I love it. This year I'll play Junior 1st for Karori . . . I run to practise every night.*

Mitchell remembers admiring poems by Yeats ('An Irish Airman Foresees his Death'), Keats ('Ode to Autumn') and Shelley ('Ozymandias') as well as songs from Shakespeare's plays. At sixteen he fell in love: *I discovered (in January 1956) that I, too, 'was human, and capable of love'. So I developed a phone call a night habit (which at one stage threatened to tie up the local phone box completely); returning home, moody, disconsolate, to complete my 'prep'.* Then came the discovery of Shakespeare's sonnets, in which he found *one or two lines that made immediate sense, were wise, & immediately attractive.*

He was an above average student, though his English marks were not remarkable; in French classes he acquired a lifelong affinity with *la langue*. It was in the school magazine, the *Wellingtonian*, that his first poem was published. It is called 'Dying Planet' and, in his 2009 recall, was about *pollution . . . asphyxiation of the whole planet.* Like all of those who experienced the Bomb as children, he feared for the earth and was a kind of urban greenie before the term was invented.

By the time Mitchell left Wellington College at the end of 1957 he had composed more than thirty poems, never printed and now gone: *aaah, what's the use . . . I may be best advised to list the poems I thought about, many of them out loud, & wrote & in some cases promptly lost: here they are:* 'The Casa Pepe Stomp', 'The Christchurch Ferry Blues', 'Wailin' at the Casa Fontana', '*Tête à Tête* Table Talkin' Hand Jive Blues', and more. These works that survive only as titles *had been read aloud to audiences, in the Tête à Tête, Rendezvous, & Man Friday cafés, to my mother at home & to some of my school fellows.*

Lawson's ballads, Shakespeare's sonnets . . . and jazz: *there was always the jazz programme on the old columbus steam radio; especially 2YC djs thursday nites. which I extended with the aid of an old pair of brushes and sticks, drum practice ! à la Shelley Manne, Joe Morello right there on the kitchen table, with a sheet of newspaper over the scoured deal planks, white with use, scrubbing and regular abrasives . . . the poem followed, usually quite easily, in sharpened pencil in a school exercise book . . . and replete with de rigeur modish avoidance of Capitals; a 'lower case' Affectation I'd acquired from I don't really know where, perhaps e. e. cummings, perhaps certain sleeve notes on record covers; perhaps just a nod towards the general stylistic novelty of the fifties canon.*

On the back of an end-of-school photo of two young men in the snow is the self-description: *looking rather bohemian.* He addressed letters to a girlfriend *Dear Bohemieeeene* and read the French poets: Villon, Baudelaire, Rimbaud. There were the Americans too. Jack Kerouac's *On the Road* (1957), with its questing, questioning and experience-based beliefs, helped define the attitudes and aspirations of Mitchell and his cohort, then entering Wellington Teachers College. His lecturers included poet Anton Vogt and charismatic painter Paul Olds. Olds held poetry workshops at his home on Saturdays, to which Mitchell, Paul Gray, Gill Ward, Don Barrier, Roland Vogt, Ian Rockel and Maureen Birchfield came. Most of these also contributed to the training college poetry magazine *Matika*.

He attended Victoria University in 1958 and '59; graduated from teachers college in 1960; and immediately began his probationary assistant year at Upper Hutt Primary School. He was still living at home, in Boston Terrace, under his mother's watchful eye. Barry Lett was at the Mitchells' one night with a group of friends Etta did not approve of: *she climbed the stairs, came in and sprayed each of us individually with fly spray; Dave said don't go, so we didn't. About half an hour later we heard her heavy step again on the stairs: she had made us soup.* Kevin Boon: *It was mandatory to contribute to the paintings, sketches and graffiti on the long low ceiling of Mitchell's attic room: a poor man's Sistine Chapel.*

He hung with the cool guys, Gill Ward said. *The first time I saw him he sat behind a drum set in the common room in a plain white T-shirt with crew cut and dark rimmed glasses—straight out of an American movie. I have an undying recollection of David running down Upland Road after a student by the name of Helen Peterson shouting: 'Helen Peterson, Helen Peterson, I love the shoes your feet is in.'* Paul Gray remembered how *he was always given to letting rip impromptu offerings but they were on the fly . . . pubs . . . coffee bars . . . parties and street raving and sometimes frothing . . . when he knew he was onto something and couldn't bottle it in . . .*

THEN THERE WAS ANNA MIRAMS. She was the daughter of Gordon Mirams, the chief film censor, who in the aftermath of the 1954 Mazengarb Report (*on Moral Delinquency in Children and Adolescents*) banned *The Wild One* and *Rebel Without a Cause*. David and Anna were young lovers; when in 1959 Anna left with her family to a UNESCO posting in Paris, their relationship continued by letter. It was a conversation on Sartre, Sagan, the Sorbonne and the bookshops along the Seine. Mitchell: *April in Paris? Chestnuts in blossom? Holiday tables under the trees?* Anna: *You have never in your life seen so many bohemians in one place. The girls never wear lipstick, only eye shadow. Have you still got your beard? I hope so . . .*

It was Anna who drew Mitchell to Europe and she remained a presence in his poetry, if not his life, for many years. On 20 August 1961 Mitchell wrote to her in Paris: *There have been many strange things happening here, and I have been most tense lately. Afraid uneasy depressed, nervous jittery and sick. I have made the most important discovery of my life as regards writing—literary discovery—and so have been under some very considerable mental strain. . . . I know now that I must proceed in a certain direction with my writing . . . I must explore my own inner universe, that strange exciting*

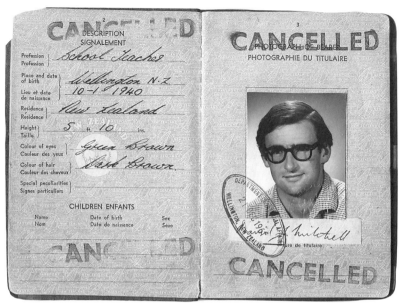

country beyond the soul and in some degree attempt its expression. I will come to Europe early next year.

It was late November before Anna replied: *This letter is going to be hard to write & should have been written a long time ago . . .* Time, distance and a legionnaire fighting in Algeria had done their work. Less than a month later, on 21 December, Mitchell's passport was issued; the photograph shows a self-possessed young man, setting out to see what he could make of the world and what the world might make of him. *I left Wellington in January 1962 to hitch hike to Auckland, from where I caught the Sitmar liner the m.v. Fairsea for a 5 week cruise to Southampton for which I paid 80 pounds sterling with money that I had saved from my teachers salary & latterly as a labourer in the meat works.* He had twenty pounds in his bank account. At Naples another pound arrived from his mother and he used it to catch the bus to Pompeii.

Fifteen poems out of a collection entitled *Day & Tide* had by this time been completed, and at least three published, including 'POEM FOR MY UNBORN SON' in the *New Zealand Listener* of 13 November and, unusually, another, 'Magpies', the following week. Monte Holcroft was the editor and in those days the *Listener* paid for poems at a guinea apiece. The early poems are conventional, but with intimations of the remarkable transformation Mitchell would make once he reached London. At the end of the poem 'day & tide' he asks if he can smile and answers himself: *i can afford to   can't i ? / that's the insurmountable joy of it !* He could, and he did.

WITHIN DAYS OF DISEMBARKING HE HAD WORK, casual and relief teaching in the provinces and in London. On 1 April he went to Paris to see Anna and thence, as 'The Singing Bread' recalls, onwards: *rocking under the erotic cradle of grief / in a beat up / purple peugeot 203 / heading south.* By May he was in Spain, visiting Barcelona, Valencia and Alicante where, another poem tells us, he ran out of money and headed north towards the French border. Through June and July he travelled in Germany and the Low Countries; by August he was at Dunkirk waiting for a boat to Dover.

By the northern autumn he was in London; a typescript records a reading at the Montmartre Café in Finchley Road, *'a blue cloak' / (song, silence, & fugue) / by d. j. mitchell / performance poems / september / october / 1962*; and another is extant for a separate set of performances at The Troubadour in Earls Court over the winter of 1962–63, where he performed with *THC Davis (acoustic guitar) / A (Boots) Perry (amplified blues harps) / & self (bongoes, congas)*. At The Troubadour he read a mix of contemporary London poems with earlier works from *Day & Tide* and at the Montmartre from the sequence 'night through the orange window'. Both these programmes, clearly reconstructed after the events, list works read, the accompaniment and the musicians, dancers, a waitress and others who performed. Boots Perry was a good friend; he turns up later, twice, in 'The Singing Bread'.

Mitchell *had a talent for meeting people*; there are lists: Tom Courtney, Sasha Distel, Dizzy Gillespie, Françoise Hardy, Mike Horovitz, Erica Jong, Janis Joplin, Kitaj, Roy Lichtenstein and many more. And Bob Dylan. Dylan made his first visit to London in December 1962 to act in a BBC teleplay called *The Madhouse on Castle Street* and stayed on to play some gigs, for instance at The Pinder Of Wakefield, a pub near Kings Cross where legendary folkie Ewan MacColl held court. Mitchell found Dylan sitting on his, Mitchell's, bed during a party at the house in

Broadhurst Gardens, East Finchley, where he lived. Paul Gray: *the way Mitch told it to me then was more or less: Who are you man? / Oh, I'm Bob Dylan. / What do you do? / Oh, I sing a bit, write a bit. / Hey . . . that's cool. So do I . . . allow me to read you a couple of mine . . .* Dylan is said to have told Mitchell to get a harmonica, which he did; but not, Gray underlines, lessons in how to play it.

In 1963, still living in Broadhurst Gardens—*a large old house . . . with a bunch of bohemians and eccentrics, all artists or students*—Mitchell met Elsebeth Nielson, the woman who became his wife. She was a young Danish au pair, remarkably beautiful, who was in London working for a wealthy Jewish family. *He was standing on top of a table, wearing a bowler hat and reciting poetry. The place was The North Star in Finchley Road, a smoke-filled dank and hopsy pub, crowded with people from all corners of the British Empire. 'You,' he said and sought me out with a piercing stare, 'Where're you from?' When I told him I came from the birthplace of Hans Christian Andersen, he immediately launched into a rendition of 'The Ugly Duckling'* (the Danny Kaye sung version from the 1952 Sam Goldwyn biopic)—*only he gave it a twist at the end. 'The duckling,' he said seriously, 'must leave the barn-yard to see things for what they are and she must also suffer a lot, before she can grow into a beautiful swan!'*

Walking home that night Mitchell picked Elsebeth a red rose and in the cold, penurious months that followed there was always a rose in a vase on the table. They were married on 24 August in the Hampstead Registry Office and honeymooned with Elsebeth's family in Denmark before returning to London. Elsebeth was already pregnant. *We rented a large bedsit, furnished with stuffy old couches that smelled of rot and animal glue. A thin layer of green mould covered the walls. And when we used the gas heater it gobbled up coins at an alarming rate, yet we never could dry out the enormous room . . . We would hold dinner parties for each other of the split pea and porridge variety and set the table with candles and flowers, still mostly stolen, then make up the characters we would become for the night.*

Elsebeth was intrigued by Mitchell's stories of life in New Zealand. *I had an uncle in Copenhagen who was the manager of a large shipping company with cargo boats going around the globe. I wrote to him and asked if we could work our passage to New Zealand on one of his boats. The answer arrived that there could be no question of giving me passage, as I was highly pregnant by now, but that there was a boat leaving Barcelona in ten days and if David could make it in time, my uncle would be delighted to have him on board as his special guest, on a one-way passage to Sydney.* Then Mitchell's older brother, Ross, advanced Elsebeth an airfare so that she arrived in Wellington six weeks before her husband did. *I was met at Rongotai airport by Etta, her friends and neighbours from the state houses at Strathmore bearing placards and balloons . . . I felt like Danish royalty.*

Etta was the rock who got Else through the late stages of pregnancy, the birth of her daughter and the stressful early weeks of young motherhood. They were in the theatre, at a performance of *Show Boat*, the musical, when the first twinges of labour pains began; but Else did not tell Etta because she knew that, if she did, Etta would stop the show. Outside, afterwards, they were walking up Manners Street seeking a cup of chocolate when Else said: *Actually . . .* Her instinct proved correct: Etta halted the traffic in the street, flagged down and commandeered transport to rush Else to the hospital. Sara was born in Wellington on 20 March 1964.

Mitchell, hitch hiking, was late for embarkation on MV *Himmerland*, delaying the sailing by eight hours; on the first night he so antagonised the captain at his table that he was sent down to eat with the crew; on the second he got into a fight with some sailors and was confined to his cabin. The captain telegrammed Else's uncle, for advice, and was told to keep the madman locked up for the whole journey. The poem that describes that *slow trip above Atlantis* doesn't however suggest that Mitchell spent the entire journey—*Barcelona, Freetown (Sierra Leone), Kpeme (Togo), French Togoland, Port Kembla (Australia)*—in the brig.

THE FAMILY STAYED WITH ETTA IN WELLINGTON for a short period during which, the story goes, Mitchell one night in error climbed intoxicated and amorous into the marital bed and found himself embracing his mother not his wife. He took a teaching job at Titahi Bay, and found a small weatherboard state house *on top of a bald brown hill, where the wind howled day and night.* His anarchic, intuitive, compassionate nature was something to which children responded; he was a generous teacher who never stayed for very long in any of the many schools where he taught; a gypsy poet on the move. He thus lived a double life, half in the classroom, half in pubs, cafés or at parties, not always on the last bus home. Mark Young: *Wellington in those days was, though small, a very active city; & because it was small, anybody who was into anything soon got to know everybody else who was also into something. The musicians knew the painters knew the poets knew the actors knew the gays knew the dopesmokers knew the dancers.*

By 1965 many of those who made up the scene were moving to Sydney; Else went, with Sara, in the middle of the year and Mitchell followed a few months later. He found a flat in Orwell Street close to busy Kings Cross: by day cosmopolitan, at night frenetic with GIs on leave from Vietnam. The small block of flats also functioned as a brothel, with a pimp who lived downstairs and used an intricate bell system to manage his girls. Sometimes, when the system failed, he could be heard calling up the central stairwell for one or another of them to come down and take care of a customer. The working girls doted on Sara and would baby-sit for her any time they were free.

Else, with resemblances to Garbo and Shrimpton, caught the attention of fashion photographer Laurence Le Guay, who shot her portfolio. Within months she was the new and well-paid face of the Sydney modelling scene. Mitchell, like many aspiring writers and film makers before him, went to work in the packing room at the Australian Broadcasting Corporation in William Street. His talk on Edwin Muir went to air. One day at the mail desk he met Englishman Russell Haley, then working in Transcriptions; Mitchell told Haley to go to New Zealand. Haley did. Mitchell also recorded poems, including 'yellow room', for broadcast on the ABC.

In the summer of 1965–66 a heatwave hit Sydney, there was a garbage strike, a plague of cockroaches and rats descended on the back streets of the Cross. Sara became very ill and nearly died; it was time to make another move. Mitchell heard that there was a strong poetry scene in Auckland and went; his wife and child followed later. In Auckland they lived in Grafton Gully; in a flat on College Hill; at 10 London Street, St Marys Bay, a famous communal house; later in Sentinel Road in Herne Bay and later still in Walters Road in Mt Eden.

But the marriage was in trouble; there was tension and violence, there were affairs. In December 1966 Else left, taking Sara, and returned to

Elsebeth, Sara, Dave, Kings Cross, 1965. Photograph by Albert

Barry Lett Galleries, 1968. Photograph by & courtesy Geoff Steven

Denmark for a year and half. They tried to pick up the pieces in 1968, but it didn't work out and she left again for Sydney; there was one more attempt at reconciliation before Else had a breakdown and spent time in Kingseat Hospital. After that she left New Zealand for good—again to Sydney. She has lived in Australia ever since. Though there were many other women, Mitchell would for the rest of his life dedicate works to her.

In 1966 Barry Lett opened the Uptown Gallery in Upper Queen Street, later moving the enterprise, which he operated with partner Rodney Kirk Smith, to his eponymous gallery on Victoria Street. Here revolutionary paintings by Colin McCahon, Ralph Hotere, Milan Mrkusich and others were exhibited and here riotous poetry readings were staged; usually with live music, sometimes a band. Dave Mitchell and Mark Young were a double act: *Mark played intellectual Baudelaire to Dave's anarchic Rimbaud,* Ian Wedde remarks.

There were many other performances during these years including, at the University Arts Centre in Grafton Road, a slide show with associated poems, followed by a dada play called *Burning Bells*. Flâneur Brian Bell

reported: *A solo performer, David Mitchell garbed in The Motley, read verses that pingponged between whimsy and droll egocentricity . . . his music hall clowning struck home to the uneasy audience.* There were publications too. The magazine *Love Juice* came out (one issue only) in 1969, with Mitchell's 'maltese jack' in it; the same publisher, the Poet's Co-operative (actually Mark Young), in the same year brought out *The Orange Grove*, a sequence written out of the visit to Spain early in the decade.

Mitchell worked up other poems from the European experience over the same period, using letters he had written to Paul Gray from London to revise 'The Singing Bread'. In May of that year the Frontal Assault Readings (Brunton, Haley, Mitchell, Wedde and the Original Sun Blues Band) went off on Sundays at the Auckland University Hall. In July, *One / The Word is Freed*, including Mitchell's 'albino angels' and 'The Visitors', appeared. Sections 6 and 7 of 'The Visitors' were inadvertently transposed and, in the Kiwi Hotel, an outraged Mitchell threw a bottle at the editor, Alan Brunton. It missed.

Poetry readings were not then conducted in a reverent silence with the audience hanging on every word. Instead they aspired to emulate the form of the rock concert. A lunchtime reading by Brunton, Haley and Mitchell at the Auckland Technical Institute Hall during Orientation 1970 almost turned into a riot. The hall was packed to the rafters and when, in the finale, the three poets chanted the chorus of Haley's 'Billy Goat Gruff's Song'—*Shouting EROTICS*—the audience joined in yelling, whistling and stamping. It was the edge of pandemonium and that was the point—readings to release a spirit of anarchy and chaos.

So outbursts in the cause of poetry were not rare. Ron Riddell recalls a 1969 Vietnam War protest poetry and jazz concert at Ellen Melville Hall: *the jazz group included a tenor sax player from the States. Toward the end of the concert, the sax player in question . . . read a poem by the English poet Adrian Mitchell with the refrain that went, 'Zap, zap, zap, zapping the Cong' . . . David was incensed. He shouted at the sax player to stop reading the offending material, and as he continued reading, David picked up a chair and threw it at him. Blood on the floor. Dented saxophone. End of the evening.*

Auckland, Summer of Love. Photograph by & courtesy Marti Friedlander

from *Dying Orpheus*, 1972.
Photograph by & courtesy
Geoff Steven

During this period Mitchell sometimes performed wearing a harlequin's costume. He was the foole in cap and bells; who lived austerely. Jan Kemp was his neighbour in Mt Eden in 1972: *David's room was bare of wallpaper, down to the scrim, no carpet. Just the boards. And swept clean. One narrow bed. A wooden trestle table. A typewriter on it. A high wooden stool. His black jacket on a hanger. Few possessions . . . he was the man with the words pouring out of his mouth. Always talking, turning a line, spinning. Testing the words, turning them over in the sound space to see how they fell back on to his ear.*

PEOPLE WERE PAYING ATTENTION. Stephen Chan *first heard David Mitchell read at the Gluepot in Ponsonby and was tremendously struck by the poems from what he called his 'Pipe Dreams in Ponsonby' series. In fact, very few of these poems made it into the book. They were reworked or, in some cases, written anew; as it turned out, the final manuscript was better than anything I had expected.* Chan used his student allowance to finance the book and his Association of Orientally Flavoured Syndics published *Pipe Dreams in Ponsonby* in 1972. A dozen of the thirty-eight poems had been written during the 1960s, the other twenty-six in a burst in 1971, during which the twelve already completed poems were also revised. Rather than a selection of previously written pieces, then, it is a consciously made artefact, like a concept album.

Pipe Dreams in Ponsonby was an uncommon thing, a poetry book that was bought and read by people who did not usually buy or read poetry. It took its place on the shelves of many share houses, along with the Hermann Hesse novels, the Whole Earth catalogues, the Fabulous Furry Freak Brothers comix and the Tarot packs. It was read as a bible of hip, a compendium of cool—all the moves, and how to make them, were in it, including the lack of insistence upon any defining move which characterised the era. As Wedde says, Mitchell was *that rare event, a timely poet, an exceptional and original talent around whom poetry swung into a different dance.* The experiences written about in *Pipe Dreams* were those of a generation of men and women then coming of age.

Pipe Dreams was widely and positively reviewed, praised by Fleur Adcock, Bruce Beaver and C. K. Stead who was, in Michael Sharkey's words, *surprised that he found so much to like in Mitchell's work—the 'extraordinary bursts of joy' in spite of experiences that left him bruised, the wry humour and, most of all, the 'courage of his emotions' that aren't undermined by irony.* Arthur Baysting, the editor of *The Young New Zealand Poets* (1973), wrote *the book is so much a unity—with the poems reinforcing one another and images re-occurring throughout—that one feels that one is reading a novel and the characters are faces on any city street.*

While many noted that the poetry was for the ear rather than the eye, the book's publisher did break hard-set rules of typography and design: *Richard King, who designed the book, and I were anxious that it not only shatter the Caxton conservatism in literary terms but that it set new design standards in NZ publishing as a whole. We were the first in the country to use a new typeface, 'theme', which had just been introduced, for an entire book. And we badgered Patrick Hanly until he agreed to let us use some ink drawings to illustrate the book.*

For Alan Loney, Mitchell's text *transgressed in other ways, and particularly in his abbreviations of various words, writing them more as were uttered—the 'e' on 'the' so frequently not sounded in usage, for example. His abbreviations brought the reader back to the materiality of the written or printed word as 'a thing and not a picture of a thing'... And what of that note at the beginning of the book, that 'all the poems in this book have been read aloud in public' which was and is to me a measure of the coming to be of the poem itself. If it couldn't survive being sounded aloud, it needed changing.*

ONE CONSEQUENCE OF THE LITERARY FAME that *Pipe Dreams in Ponsonby* won for Mitchell was the envy of his peers. Peter Olds: *Yeah I was like a lot of guys, immensely jealous... Mitchell had that effect on people... I think there were a lot of males around at the time who used to look at Mitchell as something they'd like to be. He seemed to be everything that you'd imagine a poet in the seventies to be. Dave was good with the girls, he looked good, he dressed well, he spoke well... while people admired him I think they secretly envied his success.*

Another consequence was the interest of more established figures, such as C. K. Stead, who advised him to apply to the Winn-Manson Trust for the Katherine Mansfield Fellowship, in Menton in the south of France: *You have no special responsibilities except to live in Menton & write . . . I'll gladly support your application for it or any other grant. I admire your poems enormously.* Mitchell did apply and was turned down once before being awarded the fellowship in 1975. No doubt the opportunity to harvest more French material to add to earlier unpublished poems appealed; to continue the conversation with Baudelaire. Many, like Australian poet Vicki Viidikis, sensed that France was his spiritual home.

A further consequence of the successful first book was a burgeoning interest from publishers in the possibility of the new in poetry and, more particularly, in Mitchell's own follow-up collection. *Angels at the Party* was mooted (to publisher Alister Taylor) as a title for this second book, as was *Myths of Wolloomooloo*; early issues of the magazine *Islands* published a couple of poems from this series. Both (notional) books anticipated largely Australian subject matter as, in the 1970s, Mitchell shuttled back and forth across the Tasman, partly because his daughter lived in Australia but partly, too, because he found some respite from the complexities of living in Auckland amongst the complexities of living in Sydney.

Just before one of these trips, in 1971, Mitchell gave to Murray Edmond, then gathering material for *Freed 3*, a copy of 'The Singing Bread', *unpublished and unread, a not-poem of the TRIP.* This is where

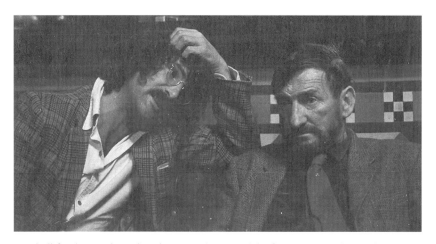

Mitchell & Glover, Christchurch, 1973. Photograph by & courtesy Keith Nicolson

the legend of *DAVY MITCHELL'S TRIP BOOK* begins, with Edmond's brief summary, in five sections, of its contents: 'The Trip' (1960–65, 29 poems); 'Blind Rooms' (1962–66, 20 poems); 'Pipe Dreams in Ponsonby' (14 poems); 'Brothers & Heroes' (7 poems); and 'Soixante-neuf' (15 poems; divorce and politics). Edmond notes that the seven poems from 'Brothers & Heroes' (*in the collection they form the centre*) had just been recorded by the NZBC but these are otherwise unknown; some of the poems from 'Blind Rooms' and 'Soixante-neuf' probably became part of *Pipe Dreams in Ponsonby*; the section called 'The Trip' must have included poems here published for the first time. Already, so early, the Mitchell oeuvre is haunted by lost works that may only be rumours; and by a weight of expectation for which the poet was not wholly responsible.

In 1973, at the University Arts Festival in Christchurch there was an epochal reading at the new Town Hall. Change was in the air, the old guard was outnumbered and outflanked by the energy of the young; though photographs of a convivial Mitchell ensconced at the bar with Denis Glover show a certain amount of generational mixing. Something like 500 people attended. Peter Olds: *Tom Paxton was supposed to be playing that night but had cancelled so they asked us would you like to use the town hall . . . what a great experience it was. We all got up and read our sombre stuff first and then pulled the plugs in the second half. Dave blew everyone away with his elegant reading . . .*

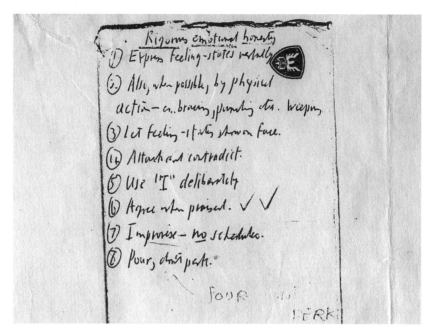

The List. Courtesy Mitchell family

THE YEAR BEFORE GENERATIONAL CHANGE of a different kind had taken place, when Mitchell ran into his old friend James K. Baxter in downtown Auckland. They had known each other a long time. *My memories of Baxter are by and large of him onstage and reading his poems aloud, to usually generous and authentic applause . . . during the late 50s,* Mitchell told students at Victoria University in 2002. *One afternoon I called in to the Lett Gallery & there was Baxter . . . He produced a poem ('Ode to Auckland') handwritten in a ball-point pen & dated & signed & gave this to me at a table in Babel Café restaurant which then adjoined the Gallery. As well as this he seemed particularly filled with advice which he figured that I, as a poet, & younger than he (I was 32) would obviously a. need; b. accept; and c. treasure. He produced a University (catholic) envelope and wrote at the top of it:*

> *Rigorous   Emotional   Honesty*

Which I personally found a little intrusive & irritating; but decided to let him rave on; and see what the result would be. He listed 7 or 8 points . . . and wrote

Mitchell & Baxter. Photographer unknown

these down on the envelope, reading them aloud to me as he did so. When
he reached number 8 he paused in his labour and looked around him (for
inspiration) whereupon his eye fell on the coffee percolating in the glass pot
on the restaurant counter. It was but the work of a moment, to complete his
list; and as he handed it to me, I read 8) Pour, don't perk ! A grand finale, as
it were, which kept us chuckling as we left and walked off down Victoria Street
West, he tap-tapping like Blind Pew, and I tossing a new cricket ball I had just
bought from hand to hand.

The next time I saw him was on a slab in the morgue.

Mitchell sent 'Ode to Auckland' to Trevor Reeves, the publisher of
Caveman Press in Dunedin (who would, in 1975, republish *Pipe Dreams
in Ponsonby*), along with his contemporary account of that last encounter:
Baxter's gone out AS IF T'CATCH A BREATH OF AIR and that hit me
pretty hard. I spent 2 hours in Babel Café Thursday before he died yakking
& drinking tea / laying it on him abt shit & mire of these islands & th hangs
a poets got t'wear etc. not complaining (you'll understand) just a good rap
as is usual with him swopping lines & jokes & all . . . a good scene. / casual,

flippant heavy as calvins arse one minute & next a cosmick guffaw & hemi
chuckle against th crass absurdities of the existential now / th fuck'd comedy /
th WHOLE ROUGH STUMBLE FOOTED TOWN th condition humaine
/ well / he ws happy enough that day and dead 3 later.

i went to the mortuary t'pay th respects & they had him somewhere, they
couldn't find him / reckoned greenlane / but I had this hunch / & finally
located him in th police section as he was DOA. I looked in through th
refrigerated haze & saw on th slabs all these pale soles & then one pair of black
filthy bastards & I sd 'that's him' . . . they wheeled him out & he looked pretty
good compared to all th other grey stiffs I can tell ya / head tilted back & a slight
smile & eyes wide open, clear & empty.

MITCHELL EMBARKED ON HIS SECOND SOJOURN in Europe with high ex-
pectations, writing to Reeves that *there's this burst of work coming on me.*
I'm ripe. He also sent a series of letters to the administrators of the Winn-
Manson Trust, pointing out that the amount of grant money offered was
inadequate to support even a single man living for six months on the
Riviera. *I was flattered . . . to get this fellowship but frankly am worried about*
financial difficulties in France. Subsequently the amount on offer was
increased but not in time for Mitchell himself to benefit; Michael King
in 1976 was the first to receive the more generous payment. Mitchell
resolved matters by *doing the Kiwi thing*: laying down his sleeping bag on
the floor of the room he was given to write in.

Before flying to France he had cut his hair short and bought a new
leather jacket in Sydney; at the mayoral reception in Menton the matrons
were affrighted; with his short curly hair and *blouson noir*, they took
him for a Marseilles gangster. While in residence at the Villa Isola Bella
Mitchell noted that there was *a continual stream of tourists, well read in*
Mansfield but woefully ignorant of NZ. I think of McCahon, Woollaston, Rita
Angus or a Robin White & how well they would look here. He did agitate, then
and later, for the Winn-Manson Trust to find some good New Zealand art
to hang on the walls of the villa.

During the course of the fellowship he performed several times with
flautist Alain Porro at the British Drama League in Monte Carlo; and
was invited to an audience with Prince Rainier and Princess Grace of
Monaco. Mitchell took the precaution of asking in advance what sort

of poems their Highnesses would like to hear and was told *something entertaining, something that would make them smile*; but, after meeting on the beach a young schoolgirl who'd escaped the rigours of preparing for her *baccalaureate*, he never made the 5.30 appointment. We don't know if this *divertissement* came to the attention of the royals or, if it did, whether it made them smile.

Thirty-seven poems from Menton are extant and at least a dozen more were logged. In the early stages they were being written at the rate of one a day. Another group of eight was written on a visit to Paris, where, broke, he borrowed ten pounds from the ambassador and took a job as a house painter. More poems came as a result of his Grand Tour, which took in *athens / rome / monaco / paris / jerusalem / london*. In Israel, Mitchell lived and worked for a time on a kibbutz; in Italy, he *saw the art treasures of Pisa Florence Rome Pompeii Capri Naples Sienna Perugia Ravenna Assisi Padua Verona Venice Milan Turin . . . nothing can touch the Pietà in the Vatican or Botticelli's things in Florence*. In London: *i amuse myself / finding exact / locations // of former / good times // amours— // time trips!* He also went to the Oval to see Australia playing England at cricket; it was 2 September 1975, day four of a six-day test match, the longest ever played on English soil.

He was ambivalent about the Menton work once he returned to New Zealand (and soon afterwards to Australia). He had everything but the second book. Most of the typescript poems have comments scrawled across them: *Reject! Revise! Keep some lines maybe . . .* Some were read aloud, for instance in the readings given with American Robert Creeley in 1976; not everyone was enthusiastic. Russell Haley commented at the time: *David is a fine lyric poet . . . he has the sharpest clearest tone in New Zealand poetry. But when he stretches that connection—when he's distanced from feeling—he can sound hollow.* Haley echoed Mitchell's own assessment of some of his earlier work as told to the Auckland *Star* in late 1974: *Much of his work in the fabled Trip Book he dismisses as documentary poetry, workshop practice, exploration.*

Mitchell remained haunted by the Menton experience for years to come, calling it *a mistake* and telling close friends like Alison McClean, mother of his daughter Genevieve, that he hadn't felt right since returning; she understood him to mean not right in his head. This may have been an early manifestation of the degenerative disease, progressive supranuclear palsy, from which he suffers. Not long after his arrival back, in 1976, his mother died. There's no indication of his response to her death nor of the effect, perhaps profound, it might have had on his mental state; but the late 'reflexions on a gift of guava jelly' may be read as a delayed epitaph for, or invocation of, Etta.

Apart from health and family issues there were other difficulties of a practical kind: with the Education Department in New Zealand, who had released him on half pay while he was in France and now wished him to work off his debt (he did); and with the equivalent bodies in both New South Wales and Queensland, where he had problems getting his qualifications accepted. Money was a constant worry. There is a dearth of composition in these years: only one poem ('th good moment') was written between 1976 and 1978.

Every writer goes through cycles of insecurity and despair, a daily tight-roping between eternity and the quotidian; in Mitchell's case, the culmination of this period of doubt and uncertainty was, in 1979, what he called *the great burn off*. What went? Everything he had written post-Menton? Or was it work from throughout his career thus far and does that then account for the 'missing' sections of the Trip Book, as itemised in *Freed* 3? Earlier in 1979 Mitchell had summarised the work he wanted to complete during a possible residency at the University of Auckland; included on that list are four books of poems, three novels, a book of short stories and a book of travel and art criticism, poetry and prose to be called *Les Cadavres Saltimbanques*. With the exception of a couple of fragments that may have been for this last, there is no trace remaining among his papers of the five prose works from this improbable programme.

As far as the poems are concerned, Mitchell's own recall is that they existed then in three alternative manuscript collections and in the burn off he destroyed what he considered the two lesser manuscripts. But he must have had second thoughts because he did subsequently restore, from memory, some of the poems that he had burned: there is a longer version of one from the Menton series, 'The Girl with Red Hair', restored in January 1980; and another work, otherwise unknown, called 'Dark Fire', also written at Menton, revised in Australia in 1978, burned in 1979, restored in 1980 and read at the Globe in 1981; on which occasion

Mitchell suggested that he might well burn it again. Annotations upon manuscripts of early work reveal that some of those poems too have been (partially) restored from memory after loss and/or destruction, suggesting a recurring pattern.

Mitchell's lifelong ambivalence about publication is echoed here. There are many stories about his reluctance to surrender work to editors. Alistair Paterson wished to publish some Mitchell poems in an anthology he was preparing. *I began trailing him from pub to pub . . . I discovered where he lived and drove round one Saturday morning . . . and finally he agreed to let me see the poems—but in my car . . . he came out with a wad of paper and got into the passenger seat beside me. There was an argument. The poems weren't really finished—they weren't ready.*

He had the wad of paper on his knee, in a nervous kind of way turning them over one page after the other as if he might give one or two to me. I reached over and took all of them from him. 'I haven't time to look at them now,' I told him. 'I'll take them away and talk to you about them later.' 'But, I don't want you to,' he pointed out. 'And I didn't give them to you.' . . . I put the papers . . . into the somewhat battered briefcase I always had with me and started the engine. He opened the car door. 'I didn't give them to you,' he said. 'No,' I told him, pushing the briefcase under the driver's seat where he wouldn't be able to reach it, 'but I have them and I'll look after them.' When Paterson's anthology, *15 Contemporary New Zealand Poets* (1980), was re-published by Grove Press in New York in 1982, Robert Creeley commented that if Mitchell had been an American, he would have been as celebrated as Ashbery, Dorn or Ferlinghetti.

After Menton there were discussions with Oxford University Press, among others, about putting out another volume of poems. OUP were enthusiastic and remained so for some years but the manuscript was never delivered. Alan Loney was going to handprint a book of Mitchell's early poems but he too was never given the works. Ian Wedde went through a series of negotiations, mostly by letter, in an attempt to represent Mitchell in *The Penguin Book of New Zealand Verse* (1985); he also never got the poems he wanted. *Oh time runs out like piss from a rusty pot*, Wedde wrote, *send something . . . Please forgive my tardy mail*, Mitchell replied. *I crawl where once I flew.* Yet he was obsessive about keeping, and keeping track of, his poems. There are lists of works, recording places and dates of composition, of performances, of publication; and lists, more poignant by far, of lost works, mostly from earlier years. Of course we all make lists—Mitchell's might have been made because he had an eye for posterity and also because he knew that both he himself and the kind of life he lived were going through irrevocable changes.

The crisis—perhaps a breakdown, perhaps an illumination—at the end of the 1970s suggested to some that Mitchell was burning out. Ian Rockel: *I wonder if the 'fuze' burned too bright at the pantheistic end. It seems as though something happened at the end of the seventies and, though he continued to write good poetry, the flame had flickered down.* Film maker David Tossman also noticed a change: *He went through some sort of personal crisis on turning 40.* Tossman associated what he thought of as a nervous breakdown with the aftermath of the fellowship at Menton. Others noted an increasing tendency towards eccentric and anti-social behaviour. In the 1980s Mitchell was banned from cafés in Mt Eden for *muttering.*

WHATEVER THE PRECISE NATURE OF THE PERSONAL CRISIS Mitchell resolved it in characteristic fashion: he turned back to performance and founded Poetry Live! at the Globe Hotel in Wakefield Street, Auckland. The venue was selected after he and a couple of friends went for a drink there one afternoon: *I was talking to the publican, a Welshman* (John Ricketts) *and told him we were looking for a place to read . . .* A general invitation was issued: *More than ever, this pretty globe, this bluegreen sphere, mother earth, spaceship earth, needs every poet it can get (and as I have always believed) needs them vocal, public, real; reading their works with whatever language, inflexion, nuance, bravura, whimsy, wit & serendipity, the times demand and their insights and skills allow.*

Iain Sharp was part of *a loose—and occasionally evanescent—circle who got to know Dave when he was running the weekly Poetry Live sessions on Tuesday nights at the Globe Hotel . . . he told me once that he was embarrassed about not producing a new book after he returned from being the 1975 Katherine Mansfield Fellow in Menton. Setting up Poetry Live was his alternative—a way of giving something back to local literature . . . there was a core of decency, even nobility, that drew people to him and made them love him . . . He was like a grumpy brother whose approval we continually sought.*

POETRY LIVE

David Mitchell
at the Globe...

EVERY TUESDAY 7-10pm

GUESTS THIS WEEK

JAN KEMP   ALISTAIR PATERSON

$2   **GLOBE HOTEL WAKEFIELD ST** $2

Unlike the collectively run readings of the Sydney Poets Union in Balmain, which Mitchell attended in the late 1970s and which probably inspired Poetry Live, the Globe was a one-man organisation. Mitchell opened up and hung the Dean Buchanan (a portrait of Rimbaud), Phil Clairmont (*The Holy Family*) or Pat Hanly (an abstract) backdrop before which everyone read. He placed the newspaper advertisements, walked the suburbs and put up the posters; it was he who selected and paid the guest poet ($30, the PEN minimum). Most evenings began with recordings of classical music—Vivaldi was a favourite—and musicians, including Mitchell's then teenaged daughter Sara, now a singer/

song writer and recording artist in Sydney, regularly took the stage. Mitchell would make announcements: the first day of spring, Wilfred Owen's birthday, International Working Women's Day; he would vary the programme, for instance staging a Lorca evening with readings in Spanish, with guitar, from the works of Pablo Neruda and Víctor Jara. On another occasion he cancelled the poetry reading to show a film about the dwindling rain forests. Usually he read last, sitting on a bar stool before a microphone with a stack of manuscript on a low table beside him.

Poets in their infinite variety were attracted to the Globe. The husband and wife tag teams, the bush balladeers, the Tristan Tzara wannabees. Voiceover men. The irascible and prescient Herman Gladwin. Entire English Department common rooms—though not all at once. China West. Those who would read once and never again. Those who came for one night and never left: all of whom Mitchell dignified as *fellow workers*. Everyone came: Barrier, Campbell (Alistair), Campbell (Meg), Duncan, Edmond and Edmond, Eggleton, Ensing, Gray, Habib, Hoskins, Johnson, Johnston, Kemp, Kidman, Macnamara, Morrissey, Mutton, Olds, Orr, O'Leary, Pule, Roberts, Rockel, Shadbolt, Smither, Stead, Tuwhare, Vogt, Wedde; former Auckland mayor Sir Dove-Myer Robinson, Queen Street flower-seller Paul, a paraplegic woman and a dinner-suited ukulele player singing his own compositions. As many as twenty poets a night: everyone, in fact, except Allen Curnow and Sam Hunt, both of whom declined to appear. Gary Mutton: *Snipers complained that Mitchell was running a coterie . . . he would be seen as a circus ringmaster getting everyone to perform tricks, insisting on his principles and his alone. Nothing could be further from the truth. David was in the business of opening doors, not closing them.*

The Globe readings were comprehensively logged and in his business diary Mitchell notes that in February 1981, slightly less than a year after they started, he persuaded David Tossman to document the events on film. Tossman was an old associate from Wellington; according to Paul Gray, Mitchell *bullied him into it . . . poor old Tosso, a sort of sensitive lost Woody Allen always about to burst into tears of destitution . . . and Groucho Mitualle snapping at his heels or wheedling and cajoling him into further folly . . . the Globe readings were dopier than the set of a Mack Sennett movie.* Perhaps they were: an application to the Arts Council for funding was declined (by telegram, from Director Michael Volkerling) so Mitchell funded the filming himself, using borrowed gear and short or long ends of film scrounged here and there.

He took out a loan of $1000 from a finance company, with his brother Ross as guarantor, and wrote to film maker and equipment provider Dale Farnsworth: *I understand from David Tossman that we will be able to use film stock, tape recorder etc. each Tuesday at a fixed rate . . . the whole deal to include transfer & on credit until the initial shooting is completed. I have no financial backing and am making the first part on my own initiative. I will have double salary cheque in August, however, and do undertake to pay your fees before we continue.* The Mitchell–Tossman enterprise was plagued by many technical and financial difficulties; but the footage that survives (about seventy minutes, with sound) is high-class documentary of a series of unique occasions. The voice recordings too (made separately in the old style) are an inestimable resource, even though, where there are images, they are not in sync with the film and the task of marrying the two has not yet been completed.

Filming the Globe was another of the many attempts Mitchell made to take poetry off the page. There had been the London shows at the Montmartre and Troubadour; in 1966 he performed 'let me here give praise & tongue' (an early version of 'at pakiri beach') with chorus, dancers and flute improvisation: *io, io, io, io / stamp sand clap hand.* There was the slide show that Brian Bell saw; a 1974 plan to stage *a mixed media three night stand . . . drama / music / light show / dancers / et al*; and the performances with the flautist in Monte Carlo. Another proposal intended to document, using *colour video,* an event to be called Wintercheer, a precursor of the State of the Nation tour. Martyn Sanderson recalls what Mitchell said of Alan Brunton: *Another poet seduced by the painted whore of theatre.* It sounds pejorative but perhaps is not: Mitchell might have meant to include himself amongst those who had, or might, succumb.

FOUR MONTHS AFTER THE GLOBE READINGS BEGAN, the State of the Nation tour kicked off, this time with the support of the Arts Council and so, trailing the paraphernalia—press kits, itineraries, budgets—of a state-supported enterprise, poetry with a backbeat went on the road. Ian

Wedde recalls: *Alan Brunton and I organised . . . a ramshackle touring show with a band* (The Four Gone Conclusions) *consisting of Bruno Lawrence on drums and alto saxophone, Bill Gruar on bass, Wilton Rogers on guitar and anything else he could get his trembling hands on, and Dave Mitchell's daughter Sara as a chanteuse. The poets were Brunton, myself and Dave Mitchell. It felt like, and probably was, a last rites for the male egoism that had seemed fresh back in Barry Lett's in 1969.* The tour began in Auckland and finished in Wellington, taking in ten provincial centres along the way. It was sometimes a riot. After the inaugural performance at the Maidment Theatre in Auckland, still high on the freed word, a group of outraged musicians and punters led by Bruno Lawrence took on over-zealous police at the Windsor Castle in Parnell. Four of them were arrested and thrown into jail for their defiance, including Bruno, who had to be bailed before the tour could leave town.

Bill Gruar thought he *should have thought more about it, I mean what on earth would the Queen or her agents know about jazz, poetry and the rigours of three weeks booze, dope and the road? Nothing, nothing, nothing . . . I had stumbled into another version of entertainment hell . . . I was in a band with no structure, no tunes, unfamiliar poetry being read aloud from the front of the stage and badly repeated through the out-back monitors, lights in our eyes which didn't matter as there were no charts to read, and somewhere out there a real live audience.*

There were other, stranger, intimations. Wedde again: *Coming back to the motor camp after an off-the-chain performance in Gisborne, Dave Mitchell saw aliens by the side of the road. They wore cowls or hoodies and long overcoats, and after the van had passed them he looked back through the rear window and saw that the cowls were filled with blank darkness with two glowing red dots for eyes . . . Dave paced up and down all night. I tell this story not to mock but to register a moment when the high poetic enterprise and romance of the late sixties seemed to drain away and be replaced with morbidity and dread.* There was a cultural shift at this time, away from the bohemian, self-indulgent, romantic model of the artist towards a cooler, more professional ethos.

Since 1972 Mitchell had been applying for grants, residencies and fellowships of various kinds, and continued to do so through the rest of the 1970s and for most of the next two decades as well; but, after

Menton, he never again received state patronage of any kind. Certainly the failure to publish a book after *Pipe Dreams* was a factor here but it may not have been the only one. He was not the kind of person the state corporate entities then rising felt comfortable having as one of their representatives. He had no patrons left, nor favours to call in; his attempts to present himself as a candidate for residencies and grants were elaborate yet askew, almost apologetic; as if he knew he was persona non grata but could not quite believe it.

ONE TUESDAY NIGHT IN MAY 1983 THE POETRY LIVE faithful arrived at the Globe to find that Mitchell had not, as usual, come before them to unlock and prepare the venue. He had walked away, three years after he began the readings, and was never to return. A month previously he had fallen in love with a 23-year-old equestrian, Virginnia King, who was training the horses for Bruno Lawrence's latest movie (*The Heart of the Stag*, 1984), then being shot in Te Kuiti. Bruno invited him down to the set, he went, met the equestrian, returned briefly to Auckland and then set out on a road trip whose eventual destination was a reading in Dunedin organised by Chris Moisa. Mitchell refused the offer of an air ticket and hitch hiked instead, re-visiting Ginna in Te Kuiti, family in Taupo and old friends down the island; hob-knobbing with Spike Milligan in Wellington; then heading down the east coast of the South Island to Dunedin, arriving at the reading just as the support poets concluded and the impresario was looking anxiously around for his headline act.

In Christchurch he stayed with Barry Southam: *Dave Mitchell called by still doing the romantic image thing of beatnik poet on the road and in love. Rang from the railway station at 9 p.m. with $6 in his pocket en route to Dunedin seeking a bed. He stayed the night after raving away in his style, wonderfully entertaining, before crashing having used up all his energy in Wellington with Ian Wedde and company. This morning I woke him at 11 a.m. and he spent another couple of hours reading his latest poems and telling us his tales of being lovestruck in Te Kuiti . . . He has written her a poem and letter every day since he departed and even sent her a long poem-telegram from the middle of Cook Strait on board the inter-island ferry.*

After the Dunedin reading he went through Central Otago and up the West Coast, thence to Nelson and Picton: documenting the trip in the eighteen-poem sequence 'Poems to Ginna', which culminates in a ballad that the *Listener* published, 'Armageddon / Hokitika Blue' and a 'Sonnet at Brightwater', which was also sent as a telegram to Ginna from the inter-island ferry, this time on the way back to the North Island. The entire trip was a quixotic and romantic quest for poetic renewal—one which was, at least for the duration, a success.

For the next year Mitchell was employed as a relieving teacher at Ruapehu College in Ohakune, apparently the one time in his life he taught at a secondary school. And then, over the next decade and a half, first in Auckland, later in Wellington, he dedicated himself to completing the university degree begun in the late 1950s, abandoned for two decades, then resumed around the time of the crisis in 1979. Triumphing over health issues and many other adversities (his attitude to academia was a volatile mix of awe, resentment, shyness and belligerence), he graduated Bachelor of Arts from Victoria University of Wellington in 2002. These were years of penury and increasing isolation: few public appearances, some memorable; many unsuccessful job applications; copious list-making; usually unanswered requests for work for publication. Most of the writing after 1984 is critical prose, often perceptive, always eccentric, never dull; some in French. There are not a lot of poems and none dated later than 1994.

A sequence addressed to *Nameless Beauty* followed the 'Poems to Ginna'; but much of the later work is a mix of glossolalia, invocations, spells, song lyrics, beatnik dada. There is a marked impoverishment of vocabulary, a noticeable increase in repetition. A curious technique emerges (earlier explored by Martyn Sanderson) in which the title of the poem expands and, in one late example, overtakes the poem. It is 'A refusal to write, in the first instance, a last minute poem for Poetry Live (after D. Thomas & J. Cage)' and in its ultimate version the title goes on for twenty-one lines; but the poem itself is a blank rectangle beneath an infinity sign.

When, at a celebration of the *Big Smoke* anthology in Wellington in 2000, Mitchell was invited to read, Sanderson recalls that *he stepped forward, studied a page of the book, frowning slightly, for what seemed a considerable time. And then stepped back, in silence, and sat down. It was a more memorable performance than if he had read a poem: I couldn't decide whether it was a deliberate statement.* Ian Wedde thinks it was: *he stood silently on the little stage in the bookshop and, whether he was able to speak or not, seemed to choose rather to listen to a voice only he could hear. Perhaps it was his own, reading his own poem. Then Michele Leggott very graciously helped him from the stage. Nothing in his manner suggested he thought he had failed to perform, and therefore I concluded that he had indeed performed: his poem now consisting of a wary attentiveness, the acutely timed pauses between his spoken phrases of old extended into an artefact of total stillness.* That silence, which might then have been deliberate, is now involuntary and almost complete: Mitchell can now no longer speak more than the odd word and communicates via gestures or brief hand-written notes.

SILENCE WAS ALWAYS A SALIENT QUALITY OF Mitchell's poetry: not the silence of absence or self-abnegation but one replete with the crackle of possibility, like the anticipatory or recollective pause before and after a lightning strike. In the work of the poem, especially as read aloud, he sought a dynamic equipoise between what was said and what would remain unspoken; the variations of the drawled-out *aaannndd* became an aural indicator of a bridge across this silence; while on the page this role is usually assigned to the *&* but might also be fulfilled by the *yeah* or sometimes, more rarely, the *ahem*. You can see a trace of this poetry of silence surfacing early on, in 'POEM FOR MY UNBORN SON', in which the advice of the court jester figure who speaks includes: *better than chanting a mime / through your carousel years / . . . steal away boy.*

Chanting a mime is a potent and paradoxical image of what Mitchell did in fact do for thirty years. It is of course a contradiction: how do you chant what is by definition mute? One of his masks was Harlequin from Commedia dell'Arte, by tradition physically agile but mentally slow and ruled by his passions: food, sex and fear of his master. In Mitchell's version he is *contra* all established authority, wounded by love, exceptionally romantic, an avatar of chaos, finally unknowable: the putative autobiographical element in *Pipe Dreams*, upon close examination, turns to air.

In person Mitchell often recalled one of the Marx brothers, sometimes Groucho the impresario but at others Harpo, with his head of hair, his harp and his mimetic silence. Sometimes even Zeppo, the clean cut, or

Gummo the missing older brother. Paul Gray concurs: *Mitch fancied the mime and clown life on the street and sometimes made me laugh myself sick with his stupid stunts . . . nothing much more sometimes than laying a loud fart in the silence of serious people and then putting on all sorts of Mr Bean faces as he peered around at each player interrogatively as if to insist that one of them had been responsible for the outrage and he would find out who.*

Ian Wedde says that Mitchell and his contemporaries were *unabashed about the importance of poetry, sceptical of subject matter—therefore ironic in relation to content but unrestrained in relation to mode.* Mitchell himself, about the time of Poetry Live, was fond of saying *poems are easy; it's poetry that's hard,* a statement that does not immediately cohere. He could have meant that being a poet is an impossible way to make a living. He would have agreed with Christopher Logue, friend of Samuel Beckett and Henry Miller, whose late 1950s jazz and poetry recordings Mitchell had heard: *poetry cannot be defined, only experienced.* He might also have had in mind a more encompassing difficulty: poetry as a calling is arduous beyond measure, it anticipates a totality of signing that is exhaustive, it is primarily the expression of the timeless in the context of the quotidian. Or perhaps he simply meant that it is easy to make a text structure that looks like a poem, but it won't be one until the intuitive spontaneous creative spark—the angel telegram—arrives.

This links to one of Mitchell's thematic insistences, an entity or a state of being that he calls *the dream* (sometimes *the trip*), as in the poem 'melba hooks': *like these sad plaster child women / who reach out reach out / from all apertures of the dream.* This is a Baudelairean realm where it is never clear if we are in bliss or terror: perhaps both at once. Some, not all, of Mitchell's poems, set a scene in which nothing happens—the curtain rises, an atmosphere is created, the curtain falls again. Exemplary here is 'yellow room' (1966), in which two people sit in a café, perhaps in Sydney, perhaps in London, *waiting for something GREAT to happen.* It's a scene from a contemporary theatre of the absurd; from an era when expectations of social and political and personal transformation were so high and, in retrospect, so unfulfilled.

These poems that open the curtains to reveal a space in which nothing happens are not nihilistic: in that charged but empty space, in that crackling silence, the dream is given its head. Here is a stage upon which poetry, the undefined, may be experienced. As the dominant mode in the work that Mitchell produced in Menton, these poems are analogous to the early metaphysical paintings of Giorgio de Chirico, themselves theatrical sets in which something enigmatic is about to, or has just, occurred. The Menton series includes 'Dark Fire', a poem that asks who dreams us and answers, mysteriously, that the lovers *are at odds with the dreamer but at one with th dream.*

The explanation Mitchell gave, that he opened up the Globe readings as an alternative to publishing the Menton poems, thus makes sense: he was theatre manager, producer, impresario at the Globe, and the stage became the place where poetry would happen; as such he was auteur, not of the poetry itself but of the occasion upon which it would occur. As a teacher for thirty years and as an active proponent of a poetry of experience rather than of definition, he consistently championed the instinctive, the innocent, the untutored utterance over that of the formal and the formulaic; this was his gift in return for what had nourished him and, wonderful to relate, thirty years later Poetry Live continues in Auckland. One of the more incendiary figures who reads there now is Mitchell's daughter Genevieve McClean.

The intrinsic theatricality of his poetry might suggest a plot of sorts. The stage that was crowded with figures and actions in 'The Singing Bread', upon which the sexual, political and romantic dramas of *Pipe Dreams* are enacted is, by the time of *Myths of Woolloomooloo*, beginning to be inhabited by figures out of history or mythology—the boy singing *helios* as the golden girl walks down the street in 'diana'; Henry Lawson and Dame Nellie Melba; the labourers in the fair smile of mother earth. In the Menton poems these figures become archetypes: an artist's model, immigrants out of Africa, nameless workers, street kids. If the earlier poems, up to and including those in *Pipe Dreams*, are haunted by time as that which takes away and destroys, those he wrote in Australia and at Menton are troubled—if that is the word—not by time but by eternity; while the performance poems that end this selection seek a way out of that dilemma in *chanting mime.*

Mitchell was eclectic and allusive, his poems are full of echoes, homages and embedded quotations; yet he is never anyone but himself. What may be his masterpiece, 'The Singing Bread', written before he was thirty years old, is unimaginable without precursor poems, notably Allen Ginsberg's *Howl*; but it does not sound like *Howl* and its refrain—*where, where are they now?*—recalls François Villon more than any of the Beats. Many readers have noted his affinity with the Elizabethan poets, which is both technical and thematic: Mitchell's preoccupation with masks and what may lie beneath them, his fear of time, his profession of *love //* & *love / & love alone* as the highest value, his foole's cap, all align him with the sonneteers of the late sixteenth and early seventeenth century. He liked antique spellings of common words (*delyt, grene, speke, werlde, werke*) and is also a poet who often rhymes; some of his seemingly free-form poems are exploded sonnets.

The other traditional form he wrote in was the ballad, learned perhaps at his father's knee or from his readings of Villon and, before him, of the makars and the troubadours. He is, certainly in 'The Singing Bread' and intermittently afterwards, a goliard figure, *a wandering student, disposed to conviviality, licence, and the making of ribald and satirical songs.* Behind that there is an older, deeper though vaguer and more fragmentary inclination to echo the poets of ancient Greece, as in the poem 'th lesson' and his later 'Pindarics'. None of these affinities, sympathies or predilections should be overstated but it is clear that Mitchell, an exceptionally pure lyric poet, was always mindful of the long tradition of which he was a part.

On the other hand popular music, especially the jazz of the 1940s and '50s, and the folk of the late 1950s and early '60s, was intrinsic to the way he wrote and performed: *but back then , it ws guthrie / we listened to , woody / & cisco houston & ramblin' jack / elliot / & janis & jimmie & morrison like / jim / hot from the van* ('Elegy in a City Back Yard'). You could construct a similar list of jazz musicians: Fats Waller, Woody Herman, Gerry Mulligan, Charlie Parker, Dizzy Gillespie. Mitchell as a performer was intense yet low-key, a murmurer not a shouter, a master of the significant pause; a voice, Wedde writes, *growling, entreating, whispering, breathing, mocking—into the delighted, affrighted ears of individual audience members.* In general, however rhapsodic the verse might seem on the page, his deliberately flat delivery emphasised irony and even disenchantment.

Mitchell reading, c. 1971. Photograph by & courtesy Geoff Steven

He could be deadpan in that dada way: filmed at the Globe, about to read 'always merrie & bright', his elegy for Henry Miller, he takes from his pocket what looks like a table tennis ball and hits it into the audience with the bat in his other hand: except the 'ball' is an egg that shatters and spatters the audience—and the lens of Tossman's camera—with shell and yolk and albumen. (Miller on ping-pong: *The importance of this recreation lies in preventing intellectual discussions.*) In another filmed sequence Mitchell reads a love poem with a rose between his teeth. Iain Sharp remembers him reciting to a group of Rotarians with a finger shoved up one nostril for the entire time he was on stage. When he stood up at the Nambassa Festival in 1979, his first words were: *Fuck Muldoon!* These impulses could surface in other ways: asked for a biographical note by Grant Duncan for *Poetry New Zealand 6*, he sent a Duchamp-like readymade—a stroke-by-stroke cricket scorebook log of D. Mitchell's 110 not out made for the Grafton Club sometime in the 1980s.

Cricket was poetry, Mitchell said, and he kept playing the game until 2002. But he didn't write much about it: the impromptu game in 'The Singing Bread' and a brief reference in 'la condition humaine' are the only two examples in this selection. To play the English game outside the Louvre (which he does not at first recognise) was a beautifully transgressive act; the barbarian at the gates of culture. Cricket can also be a game of miracles. Mitchell once took a hatrick bowling his *little floaters* on the Devonport #2 ground to win the game for North Shore: off the last three balls of the last over of the last match of his last season in Auckland. The penultimate ball of that extraordinary over was described by cricket writer and fellow player Roger Brittenden as *a geometric figure of mystical significance*, which makes it sound like a line of verse. There were many such lines that never got written down.

In another place, only half jokingly, he lists his influences: *Zilpha Kershaw, Shakespeare, The Bible, John Keats, Donald Duck, Franz Kafka, Groucho Marx, e. e cummings, Fairburn, Zeke Wolf, J. K. Baxter, Judith Wright, Banjo Paterson, Bob Dylan, Henry Lawson, Marilyn Monroe, Jacques Prévert, Glenn Turner, Horace, Clara Schumann, Pindar, Anne Frank, Jesus Christ and Michael Joseph Savage.* His statement in *The Young New Zealand Poets* concludes: *yet, still th same crass questions / how come this is th way yr time's spun / as if ALL 'ART' were not gratuitous / as if th 2 modes*

Auckland, c. 1986. Photograph by & courtesy Nigel Roberts

/ *celebration & therapy (according to the manic swing) were not universal /*
as if the poem itself were not th holy erasure of just this manner of barbaric
enquiry! Th act is older than th question / thereby negates it. Literature,
Mitchell once told Michael Morrissey, *is not important. It is the look in a*
man's eye that's important.

Examination of his manuscripts suggests that performance was so
much the essence of Mitchell's approach that even the writing down of
poems was a pre-performative act, like a composer scoring a piece of
music. Where, as a consequence of revision for live performance, two
versions of the same poem exist, they seem to have been regarded as
separate works. The apparent contradiction between a poet who was so
difficult to publish, who so rarely let his work out into the hands of editors
and publishers, yet one who carefully preserved those of his manuscripts
that he did not burn, might be resolved here: the poems exist in their
ideal form only when performed and so the scripts were valued primarily
as scores; once they had been published, they lost their mutability, their
charisma, their ability to transform.

This was Alan Brunton's opinion: *Language is a performance. The pleasure is in speaking, that's where life is. Writing is a kind of death, the plague, a dis-ease.* Brunton also wrote retrospectively of that moment four decades ago when *Imperial Standard English whistled to a stop . . . Mitchell's* Pipe Dreams in Ponsonby *was central to the abandonments of decorum that followed . . . battlelines were drawn up between opposing mythopoetries. Tragedies of history and geography, performed by a chosen few on a cleared section, gave way to the inclusive carnival—Mitchell's myth of friendship. His ampersand, &, was the sign of the neoteric as was the lowercase i of the harlequin—taking the line of most resistance, ungrateful to society.*

TO MEET DAVID MITCHELL NOW IS A PLEASURE and a surprise. He resembles the photographs of his father from the 1940s and beyond that brings to mind a dapper old European gentleman gazing reflectively upon the vacancies: that empty stage where poetry happens. He can seem remote but will respond with enthusiasm to specific questions, writing the answers down on paper; his memory is intact. Eric Beach went to see him at the place in Bronte where he lives in care: *When we go I am finally in front of Dave. He offers me his hand. Firm handshake. Smile. Eyes held. Of course during the time in the visiting room he'd whispered a laugh and a name. To endure a biographer with good humour is a sign of tolerance . . . The room is either asleep or yawning. 'Une domaine en on l'oublie les temps.' The room is 'a place where one forgets the time.' His friends are wrapping his life around him like a cloak.*

His attitude to the publication of this selected poems is untroubled; while grateful that he is at last to receive his due he seems perplexed by the long delay. When we went out to tell him that the deal had been done and the book was now certain to appear, he nodded but remained uncommunicative. And then we repeated the opening lines of T. S. Eliot's *The Waste Land: April is the cruellest month / mixing memory and desire / breeding lilacs out of the dead land . . .* Dave transformed; a grin spread over his face and he began to drum upon the table with his hands: accurate, rhythmic, syncopated drumming like that which presaged the writing of a poem at the kitchen table in Wellington all those years ago.

I / Day & Tide

A Letter

I am here my love
beneath an apricot sky.

Summer is a young girl,
her voice is thick

in these green islands.

The valley gorse was burning
last week. Quietly in the night.

Tonight it is warm. Just a song bird
and the hills.

It is not lonely, but very slow.

I am here my love.
This is all

my beauty.

day & tide

I.
today
in the small heat
of a morning courtyard
behind the sky stilled leaves
seven men sit
on seven small stools

hand chin
to elbow knee'd
while above them
in that clean blue arch
the steady sun turns to its timeless tune

before them
in the garden
lies the cool lady
spoiling in the stillness
of their regular gaze

i weep and walk down
the white chalk hill
to dine alone
at a bright wooden table
immaculate
on the beach.

2.
the tide has not quite come
and there are crescents in the sand
wind crescents
at the dry summit

round the baked rim
these thirsting elements swoon
in that blue reverence
enamoured am i of walking

the busies don't understand
the ironing board pleasure

of walking

the meet heat
of the slow solemn feet
and . . . . the sand !

3.
the tide has not yet come
and there are wet sea laps
where the lappings are

daisies !   daisies ?
           yes.   daisies in the sea.

daisies
           in the dog eared shadow
           of the daymoon

the sea, the sea, the
           lunar, lunar sea

4.
i can afford to smile though
        can't i ?
with my gullet an ecstasy
        of jingling gums

i can afford to stand on the beach
        at the limit

to toe the never settled line
        with low embarrassed shoes
and a donnegal tweed coat

silent
        with my hand a bone at my bony brow
and stagnant hair
        my eyes darting this way or that

i can afford to   can't i ?
that's the insurmountable joy of it !

POEM FOR MY UNBORN SON

My name is Yorick
and the worm
is in me
Jesting was my fancy
clowning my business
but I am sick now
the play is done

You will grow
saddest
most infinite minstrel of all
reading
playing quietly alone
hiding in the library
by sunless statues
or in the hall

Being slight and grave
your fine hands will lie
obedient at table
your great eyes black
over straight lips
washed with no smiling

Better
than chanting a mime
through your carousel years
flushed and stiff
like a red marionette
or your father at court

                    steal away boy

'old, rock clad man, sea girt . . .'

(for David Eric Mitchell
d. Wellington, 1953)

old, rock clad man, sea girt
beneath yr cobar hat &

in yr frayed & worn
studded

but , collarless, shirt

/ smiling, wanly
at this werlde's

unbelievable iniquities . . .

i just want t'say
' on yer ! on yer, digger ! '

if, from this, you
will take no hurt.

strange birth

he

was early exposed
congealed

while still
in pod

suddenly
the woman

white moss'd
death naked
lay

opened

on the river bank
like

a rut . . .

the earth   healed
he moved

peasants washed him
in fear

felt his hornéd skin
harden to shell

beneath
that coarse bathing

watched him roll up
roll away

coughing dew

filled the bright sky
with wailing

wailing against
too great

a greenness !

2. The Singing Bread

maltese jack

(soho, 1962)

greek st / 5 p.m. & shoes
like soft chimes
in the steady evening

where thin men step briskly at dusk
& eyes that watch me watching
appear

from dark windows; strangely inscribed
& newsboys perform senile shuffles
behind their sexy headlines . . .

rockel sits impassive in a café
' le macabre '
stealthily rubbing shins with some fat
mother's help; hot

out of sinister hamburg
chuckling with lust in his hearty throat
looking
       cock eyed
       & great with the elements
       like a spider shaken
       line drawing
of a FAMOUS FRENCH PHILOSOPHER !

up the crooked street the windmill girls
cross their slim legs at cast iron tables
eating saltbeef sandwiches
& drilling formica with candy nails
while watching maltese jack through the window
selling hotdogs
up high tonight / 180°

ultra polite
looking blue
            eyed & great with the elements
            like PAGANINI IN HIS PROGRESS !

later
the last tube trains gone & silent
quietly descending a HARRISON MARKS
staircase
I do hear violin music !

glimpse through the slats of a venetian blind
an ageing stripper / dancing slowly
as if alone
one hand raised to her throat
like POLA NEGRI long ago
& the old phonograph turning.

walking up fleet street to an early pub
rubbing shins with the dead tribes
in the melting snow
eyes that watch me watching appear
in shop windows / beneath strange inscriptions
in cursive script
& the thick apricot fog comes rolling in from the river . . .

velvet
yeah. like a way of life.

The Singing Bread

(paris, 1962)

french bread / ' the best in the christian world '
holds within its cells
the mysteries. yeah. the mysteries . . .

drinking / drinking great rum & pernod afternoon
with canadian music student / harmonious lush
cinzano & anis too ! yeah. the best this pagan counter

point ! nul. ' je suis au cul de l'univers ! ' bad
language . . . ½ gone under the lowlands zinc. mal

de siècle . . . appears again as a choir of angels
in the yeast
                nickel or copper ? no matter / great
                        or small / coins
                lie static on the zinc.
                        comforting braille.

the best lush this tall bar can provide. speaking of berlioz
& john coltrane. miles too !

playing cricket with a rolled newspaper & tennis ball
along beautiful / flat wicket / stone corridors
outside some grim building that looked like the louvre . . .
later found out that it was the louvre.

amerkin students too ! millions of them / all stinking rich

volkswagens & the best guitars !
fathers in metal or ' shares ' who may have mine.

& then some wild young spade chicky / pure cockney voice
from the deep sounds of barbados. yeah. its true !
but born in mile end / stratford / or was it bow ?
perpetually astonished in the breasts
great exclamation marks for nipples
beneath the ' light grey ' marks & spencer sweater
& nothing else / nothing / save the mysteries / yeah
                                        like yeast!

myself. alone. afraid. waiting on the feast of love
wandering soulful & alone / through boulevards of the mind

drunk on nothing & everything / creating great lines for
                          a religious novel called
                          ' the singing bread ' O
                          yes . . .   & pondering!

millions of lost eyes ! real gallic too ! like sartre's
whose pupils never did & never will match or flare up
against the retina's wall

                          or low barricades like in some
                          spanish painting. is paris
                          burning? is fontainebleau?
                                        is chartres?

swingers & hoods / my generation ! / I ran among them
& didn't groove / but chanced on again in summer london

good / wild / skinny / hard men & tough birds
glamorous & tinselled against the métro railings

tight about the mouth / dressed in leather / & burlap
tinselled too with harmonicas & blue guitars
along fretting cinema queues / & champs élysées / jewel bright !

buskers all ! wide eyed & shaggy / like hairy beasts
from the earth's core / from out some SF movie long ago.

holding out / holding out within the skin / & with the pale hands
for centimes & clever 'french' abuse / yeah the drab
currency of love. no bread man. called in this city 'pain'

beasts & angels / starving / suffering the ministrations
of the brave gendarmes / for love & wisdom / under no
hard helmets of 'freedom' / like japanese bachelors of politics

in the ' now '
parades . . .

under no hats / save the haloes of fear / under no hopes
save the basic & naïve / like those of children
under no stars of harmonious systems / drinking & smoking
& starving / really starving / in the streets of apollinaire

but human / all too human / as I came to know. later
in summer london / when all charing cross & hampstead heath
visions come back / come back like smoke & dream / now
as I write / yeah. human.

like lonely boots p. / 'all women are masochists'
but feeling in the deep heart / the reverse was true.

fruity cambridge accent & donnegal tweed / but boots
'of spanish leather'
tall / shadowy figure in the inevitable fog
& taut face / but beautiful soul / & where
where is he now ?

& others, too—
'hard men' a cult which was sad / but some

immediate answer then ! / like 'go into the
bathroom & wait for me'. many, many, beautiful women.

& it worked ! yeah. & I spent some time SOME TIME !
rolling joints for nervous husbands / or lovers

not afraid (you'll understand) just not sure
WHAT TO DO !

Yeah. rich / wild / yankee chicks / high in europe's
summer. coasting on sweet rails of mid west blues

but it was 'folk' then. folk. blonde chubby thighs
creased over levi strauss denim / & songs of sunshine

'keep on the sunny side always on the sunny side
keep on the sunny side of life' . . . almost always

accompanied on the AUTOharp / & the thighs too
in their creasing ! AUTO erotica ! america in earl's court
THE TROUBADOUR ! / yeah & in paris too.

now I have to say it / though editors wont believe
a poet, zimmerman / quietest of all. who sat on my bed
during a party / broadhurst gardens NW6 / 1963

singing his great poems / politely heard mine / drank
wine. was it burgundy ? / yes the greatest under worse

hangs than starvation / pain & bread. & where
where is he now ?

swingers & hoods I didn't know then / under the gas
lamps of montparnasse / but chanced on again / later

in summer london . . .

conning the youngest / the richest / amerkin gels
from the sorbonne / new guitars / by the month !

volkswagen trips / & all delights / real or invented
all delights ! like oral sex in crowded tube trains

& amplified harmonicas / electric but still sad . . .
where boots makes it at last with back to audience, man
like miles ! ONSTAGE at the marquee / oxford street
swinging with all his heart & soul / with / with /
was it chris barber's 'cats' ? ah ! jesus !

for the harmony ! for the harmony !

chez maurice. place de la contrescarpe. bar 'le nuage'
with anna. café dome with chantal

maj. / who refused to speak to me for eleven months
in england / then woke me with a kiss

ten seconds before she left for paris
with some unnameable disease . . . wearing in that moment

the wisps of pain / leaning over my broken eyes
in grim anticipation, already, of the final breaking

of the bread of life. yeah. the cellulose mask. the final disguise.

maj. weeping in her cold coffee / in puzzled injustice
at sheer pain / the weight / of it ! this time in paris frost.

drained like some, old, seaman / lingering out of time
along sepia piers / in turn of the century / stockholm . . .

drained by the bright / flesh anchor she held
in her skinny thighs / disease as slow / as serpentine

as time itself. alive only with grief / absolutely stoned !
in the jardin du luxembourg / recognising the trees as

her brothers / gone out many years / these tall seven /
calling each one by name ! & then / the sudden / the
illuminated smile ! & where

where is she now ?

whose mascara betrayed the nordic bone so perfectly
that she received a proposal from algerians & persians
& greeks & even from the french !

twice in every minute we sat there ! & from one jewboy too. yeah.

where is she now / whose face haunts me still
& whose great sullen shoes crossed over the bridges of paris
in such agony.
                        pigalle.

                                    or was it clichy ?

much later / one christmas morning / as the barges lay
trapped in the frozen / the erect canals /
' like antique weeds; never to bloom '
I saw her face / scrawled on a wall / frigid in red chalk !
like some mediaeval, woven thing !

                                    & under the inevitable
                                    bridge / a large united nations poster

saying simply /

                    ' pain '

yeah. bread. now, all french bread sings / & this too / my song.

pain ! & air ! & the frozen desmesnes
of love. / & who
will argue ? / under what banner ?
                         WHAT MANNA FOR THE WORLD
                         campaign ? / how should we recognise
                                  the brothers of hunger
                                  & green sisters starving ?

I am one / who will sing / I am one whose house is white
constructed entirely from 2nd hand doors. YET

I am one who will sing / scream the banalities
of reason.

LOVE ! LOVE !   chained at the deep heart cannot fail
                         though some prayers do not come through

love / love / as free / as cold as water / should not
be rationed / under the banners of logic !

should no longer be rationed / under the pain of death !
jesus witness if I lie / & this the text
too / of all I said to my beloved / anna

carmen lives ! in oran. the buboes have moved north !
so that ALL french bread sings

great choirs of tiny white voices
chanting life & love madrigals

from out the crisp mass. & that last
sad story / anna / was too cruel !

ridiculous figure of the boy from stratford
in taranaki / coming up & grieving to your embassy

rue victor hugo / who went to sleep that night
in an ancient sleeping bag / under the bridges of paris

singing like a heroic fool ! was bitten in the bowel
& feet / by the wolves of the frost

right foot amputated next day / a throaty chuckle
as you changed the subject / & 'some more wine ?'

undue expense for NZ / shame ! shame ! I cried
hobbling away / disguised as a tree !

yeah

& the europe I know now, seems a tight arsed whore
like goya's witches / whose once proud / unnatural
beauty

has turned in / & is growing like that ! IN IN towards
the slight bone !

but then / europe / like the dream of love
was all light & beauty
where abattoirs near clichy
at full bat / at the break of dawn
seemed love factories ! / & the métro

like a subterranean palace / filled with thorndon trams
went too slow !

eager as I was / to earn some mark in life
& frank before the gall

of french sophistication
broke my heart. ah ! chantal / anna / maj / kerstin
                                        elsebeth & june !

how could you know my need to adore ?
how could you divine my thirst ?

ah ! maria. in your tiny room
how could you know my preference

for your mother ? & the sounds of the bread
singing. / & the green green diesel buses

& the pain of life / under the clearest skies
my life ! too much . too much. & of nothing !

open as a catholic to the high
tight / clear call of th death
spirit / true love's pain. & bitter end.

open / I say ! open at last !
I sacrifice one / weird / last joint for sanity

in the sacre coeur / yes / IT'S TRUE !
the nearest heaven I've been

except later / first trip / with first wife.
dangerous ' ready to go anywhere ' light
mirrored in filthy youth hostel eyes.

& strop razor fantasy / cutting & cutting
cutting only / a demi baguette / loaf of
                        bread.
severence of the choirs / slashing at angels
yeah.
            for the harmony. for the harmony.

finally lushed up in cendras café / zinc
counter / like I said / amputee veteran

& spider wife / pinched in the spinning face
with cold & no hope ever ! also with the natural

map of the seasons. slime & sap
                       slime & sap

                                           who was once green
                                           leaf green.

made it back to montparnasse
maj buys me 2 books / one title was ' tropic of . . . '

bought a loaf / 38 centimes / demi baguette
slung against the pewter cheek of grief

like artaud's flint lock / FRENCH SOLDIER PAR EXCELLENCE !
transistorised pain in my ear.

as I score a lift / blast through this city
of love

one last time / 7.30
cafés cafés cafés cafés cafés

on to the high way south / gradually getting up
to 25 or 30 kilometres per hour   !!!

sitting up front
in the van
weeping for life . . .

not hearing the crazy, beret wearing, fusilier
driving casual as a gendarme !

not hearing nothing ! only the choirs of pain
under the weight of time. yeah. my time.

rocking under the erotic cradle of grief
in a beat up / purple peugeot 203

heading south / lost in the fugues of the bread
& ' the life '

yeah. my life. under the choirs of pain.

discarding my only possessions / a packet of gauloises bleues
!

channel steamer packet rail & boat tickets
floating out of the window

like confetti / from some dream marriage / I will make
only in the last 10 minutes / as the world winds down
self with self with self
yeah. my world. my life. my time. / confetti
like the darkest fragments of a continuing conversation
with baudelaire.

albino angels

(la jonquera / valencia '62)

bells peal
on an old rope & señor nin

starched collars / high
on th throat

like ' bat's wings '
stamps my passport . . .

but
i am lulled

by th curious sound
of spanish trains . . .

a little girl
with a hoop & a stick
is pushing the world around
beneath the pyrenees
/ is perhaps there still !

where 3 albino angels
climbed stiffly
from a volkswagen
wearing dark glasses

looking like mountains !

where françoise met her maker
for the first time in 15 years
disguised as her father
&

later / went swimming
with her unborn children . . .

where glass jars in cafés held
within their clasp
multicoloured shellfish
without their shells . . .

where a 303 cop in a cardboard hat
showed me a beautiful / dirty picture

then tried to arrest me
for bringing it in to th country !

where a young whore sang ave / ave maria
while she screwed
                          later fainted
                          at th bullfight

where most men resemble bulls
& women guitars . . .

where callow army recruits drilled hopelessly
in th main streets
wearing sand shoes & 1942 / alan ladd / twill trousers . . .

where a thousand men with short handled shovels
demolished a mountain in a fortnight . . .

where i died of a broken heart
having lived on sugar alone / for 3 weeks

where i tried to make love on a bicycle
at precisely 5 or 6 in the afternoon

achieved only th slow leak . . .

where th crazy wooden cathedral is stoned
out of its christian mind / day & night
night & day . . .

    like crafty franco . . .

ay !

  barcelona
  barcelona

  where ALL THINGS were possible
  &

  th world ws real !

VERY FLAT HORIZONS !

(Dunkirk, 1962)

It so happens
that I am tired of being the sucker
sick to death & weary with the world's foreign claws
pricking at every old scar
especially on this pier
& along these maritime boulevards
looking out over still, leaden water
etched in the evening with that green
history of madness.
                            Other suckers
old soldiers, long dead, sit up & smile
in shop windows as I pass
muttering, tapping on the pane
MAKING THE SIGNS ! . . . poor imbeciles !
who have been taken in
What does it matter to me ?
                            I
who wear no uniform / save the necktie of blood
the old braid of the lost infantry.
They will not take me in ! All flesh withers
& fabrics fade & all flags burn
though cowards fade away.
                    & with the stealthy night
                    there comes a wistful whore
                    strolling like in some bygone decade
                    through sepia stills of heroic
                    government made, movies
                    I
                    turn to her / as to some dun
                    thing, some khaki ally
                    & tunnel in & tunnel out
                    from her plush salon
                    a sweating coward but no sucker !

Up grey boulevards & push & pull along the piers of night
hunched up in the sulphur glow
of electric pinball machines
bent & double as if wounded
thinking things over & intently
pushing coins into slots & scanning the sky
over england
like in some other , coloured movie
tight lipped with fatigue
grimy / & stubble chin jutting curt, heroic

ahem.

my great old greatcoat collar turned up
against the Hollywood wind machine
. . . a grimace or 2 & the war's over
only sad & humble & weary in the flickering light
MATURE . . . . like Victor !

Ah ! They have taken me in !
I, who wear no uniform
in no greatcoat & jackboots
only an oilskin parka & ripple soled
rubber jandals MADE IN NZ
dreaming of home and wurlitzer hymns
in the crazy house of my youth
when the lights came up
& the movie was over.

Now
the ferry / like a wedge of Gouda cheese
on a billiard table
pushes out across the harbour bar
orange lead paint on the dark green sea
& I
who wear no uniform / weary nevertheless

watching the invisible rescue yachts
in the mind's retreat
sit
in the plush saloon with Lily &
Marlene
getting steadily rotten
under the inexorable advance of time

waiting for the white coast to come up
yes

the cliffs of Dover.

slow trip above atlantis

(a prayer for my daughter, 1964)

shipping passes daily
japanese fishermen
' pirates '
swung across the bow
. . . 3 grinning men
   in blue serge
   signal . . .

cheeky & camp
on the high seas
' I love you. I love you. '

our first officer / stern danish
clark gable
will not believe that the NZ govt
pays to have deer shot
thinks I am
. . . a strange one . . .
              I AM ! I YAM !

½ dead from self abuse / swung under
the tropic of cancer / & weird
daylight dreams
of homecoming
like a birth & a death . yeah. &
the sea . like the weight of so many
dead relations
on my breast . . . &

I am terrified of the sea.

now
all down the coast of africa
                   africa
sometimes visible to the naked eyes !
I listen to radio
          radio
                & I hear the tongues
                with my nude ears
& advertisements, too, in swahili !
& the beatles too, O yes. strange songs
when all alone on a glassy sea . . . like
' she loves you; yeah.yeah.yeah. '

while watching albatross come upwind
from the buried masses of the spirit

' under the keel 9 fathoms deep
  from the land of mist & snow '

gliding into great dreams of future bliss
like christian souls ! . . . christian souls !

swooping in stupendous silence over the ship.
one lands . . . it is eyeing me . . .

as I grope feebly for the transistor
& avert my unsteady gaze &
cool glance
            out
                 & over the ultramarine . . .

& I am terrified / of course !
I am terrified of the albatross.

now
all around the table mountain
I am watching the sexy , flying fishes

one day a whale . . . & thousands of miles
away
this day, my daughter is drawing her first breath
but I am pondering
lush
malcolm lowry / in his cell
' 9 fathoms deep '

& the sharpeville all
blacks / & martyrs too, all

savage african queens & all
great transplanted souls
lost lovers !   skin divers !

& all darkened suns & daughters
black & comely / & all
the authentic dead / whom sartre has named

& freedom riders too / in all lost continents
of desire. ah ! jesus ! it hurts for truth !

it makes sense too / despite cowboy kate
& the stealthy ease of the first five eighth

& the dutch massacres !

now
I am terrified of those blond angels
whose swords are of the logic of words
& those dark angels too / who persist in the myth

& I am terrified of the greatest intentions
of each & every state / & I fear their acts—
for I have learned to dismiss their words . . .

& I am terrified of the white heat influence
for ' good ' as much as for ' evil '
from out the buried cities of the flesh

& I fear their fresh schemes & compromises
& I fear their pacts & their treaties
& I fear their dreams & their lamentations
under the guises of ' love ' . . . yeah. & its all true
its all happening, under the ' blades ' of love
& ' justice ' & who can ponder for long & yet
remain, unafraid / sane / & hope to hang , to place
sweet children on the christmas tree
of this world ?

now
I'm hung up , myself, in this late blue & white day
but great / with hope
                              nevertheless I see
a city growing
' just like that ' / up
& out from the pleasant sea

a klee city
like a slow & leaning cartoon
as this day passes into night

gold for white / white for black
& this slight ship
rounds the last soft point
of the coloured cape
                              while at my back

75

a sudden sunset draws its cloak too
like orange smoke
against this fitful night & those to come !
yeah.

a sunset draws its cloak
about this steamer

in the dark blue night.

3. The Orange Grove

lemon tree

I lie
beneath the lemon tree
and the moon
through the heavy leaves

touches
      darkens me

I
come down
to where the orange lamp is

Through the beams
great moths fall
heavily

rise again

there is nothing to disturb
      the silence

I sit here
in the dim garden
for a long
      time

I know the orange lamp is lit

I see
great moths fall
heavily

rise again

I know the orange lamp is lit

I sit here unmoving

I lie beneath the lemon tree
and the moon
through the heavy leaves

touches
        darkens me

night through the orange window

(i)

Tonight
in the amber warmth
of her deeper dreaming
I will assert my seasonal self

living again
the rain and mist of her smile

so that now
in the mystery of the moment
her face
is at my delirious throat
her blind lips murmur
over my salt neck
my shoulder

so that now
in the silence
of the moment
we walk again
through that young night
and this

step by slow step
into the trembling.

(ii)

That night
and this
you leaned forward

your shoulder in the firelight
patterned
with the delicate bruising
of ferns

tenderness and tenderness and tenderness

your cool hand
was on my face
to still me
tender as a receding sigh
pale as the sound of your eyes closing

your slender hand
moves over my face
tastes my mouth
pauses at my throat to listen—
my blood
          its mad sport

your slender hand
moves over my face
to still me
as if you were blind

tenderness and tenderness and tenderness

your slender hand

at my eyes lip
and sheaves of bright hair
bend tiny
down all the slim meadows
of your autumn skin

your cool hand
moves over my face

to know the form of the formless
to print time into a frown
a petal of smiling
or a terror
too beautiful to speak

silence
is your cathedral.

(iii)

Tonight
in the vast room of this still moment
in this century
between the bell and the blue star
through the screen of shocked air
distilling voices from the street
I have you
as you really are.

Outside a star is ringing like a bell
death. day. birth. night.

I could not possess you again
save as now

you are
> the sound of heat
> in the grove
> ripening

you are
> death's first small lily
> breathless
> come in wonder

panting at the foothills
of my grey face—
And I bemused

you are
heat from an unlit fire
the scent of unspilt rain
the aftersound of music
from across the black and white lake

you are—
it is nameless
what you are
unspelt

death. day. birth. night.

Outside a star is ringing like a bell
ripples of warm panic over the poor day
his giant face.
his voice is big
through
all the heavens
calling Ulysses.

It is not that I am lonely
in the world
without you—
but that I am lonely
in you
without you

Tonight
I have you as you really are
within; without;
there are so many worlds

stacked like cards
between the bell and the blue star

who would not like the giant shout ?

(iv)

I remember her as a fifth season
she
who came unheralded
into those lean months
shaming the precise blue evenings
with the proud eternity of her flesh

she
who loved proudly
causing wonder and a little natural awe
who drew long cool fingers
slender and pale as dawn
over my thick face
who wandered singing
through my light head
scattering memories of the future
like burning pebbles
                    or roses

she
who caught my lips gently
between her small cold teeth
who kissed the husks from my slow eyes
so that I too might weep
for life

I remember her as a fifth season
who came unheralded
and walked in beauty.

Forty Words on Three 'Where's

I will go

      where

a low sun smoulders
under a weave of sky

      where

frost is a blue cloak
about the lean shoulders
of   afternoon

      where

the shore sound
of her light breathing
is a fugue
   over & against
the clasp of sleep.

SATURDAY MOUNTAIN BEAUTIFUL EUROPE
LOVELY WOMAN SUNSHINE POEM

(For Elsebeth (Nielsen) Mitchell. Dec. '67. Sentinel Road
(26) Herne Bay , Auckland , New Zealand)

Saturday mountain & morning
trees in hair like sweet marc chagall

                            in my happy window
& up my yellow ceiling this bright day !

a star of some new psalm & jolie opera
which is being written in my open self

& all along the crumbling, varicose walls of ancient Europe
newborn babe again like Blake's cool children of the mind

& its tiny cafés & streets are tinkling in the inner ear
& all that tinselled carnival of love

                      & sunshine songs

shall come
        & come again.

I break the sourness of my head at times like this
saturday mountain & singing flower awake with new

        Europe !

& while the piano downstairs sings out
& while dogs & children in the street
sing out / sing out
            early & late

& while new Europe , lovely woman , swells again
within the freedom of this dappled room

& in the light beneath the mountains of my head
memories of Essen & Hamburg & Copenhagen & Troyes
& sullen Africa
                    sing out / sing out

& while the piano down the hallway sings
& outside birds fly , singing . . .

& in the bistro of my head new
Europe flies past singing
& while the shadows of this saturday loom like love
across the ceiling of an earlier dream

(sweet marc chagall ; joli marc ; l'opera, Montparnasse)

& while the loom of love binds this new Europe
round the mountain of my steady self

till moon & stars & trees grow in my growing hair
& bells ring like kisses & tramcars & the métro sings

& the heavy diesel buses green with new youth of fragile Europe
go flying ; singing past

            THE LYRIC OF THE PSALM WILL BREAK !

will break the sourness of the head
& throat & mouth will sing
with cafés; pianos; seawalls; trains & buses & all the heavy
aeroplanes & silver bicycles along the boulevards & underneath
the chestnut trees
                    & London's iron railings too & all the charing
                    cross hampstead heath visions come back like
                    smoke & dream . . .

& while the piano down the hallway sings & dogs
& children talk to me

          & all things sing

I break the sourness of my head
& undermine the sometime grief

              at absence & the dead
              conversations of hatred

SATURDAY MOUNTAIN BEAUTIFUL WOMAN LOVELY
    EUROPE SUNSHINE SONG

I break the sourness of my head
& all that murmuring carnival
shall come & come
& come   & come again.

The Visitors

1/
In the pale evening
where dreams circle like pigeons
over fountains
one
coming lately
dressed in algebra
discerned a pause in the argument

insinuated himself with flattery
& described heaven in 4 letter words

for want
of reply

he took the flowers off the lips
of those present
& disappeared

shuffling like an old man.

where my heart pumps in slow comfort
I feel at home.
under the wooden bridges of the world
the clowns & seamen sing
traditionally at ease
in the soulful evening

fabricating momentary tents & arches
with constant hands
& tinsel bright beams
of the harmonica

I am one
who has come lately
naked
       & newly born

I am one
whose house is white
constructed entirely
from 2nd hand cast off doors

In the pale evening when all things sing
I am the one
who welcomes the strangers
saying
       cupping my hands about the words

admit them ! admit them !

2/
Coming & going & standing still
I am the world's enemy
& the stranger's friend

along the slanted banks of great canals
the feet of the lost
tread softly on stubble & wake

no dead
      echo
           in the living towns

for they, being lost,
are the world's strangers

& our kin.

        bronze they are & brass
        to the fleeting visions
        of the day

        but

        warm as blood & honey
        in the bitter night
        they tread with feet of flowers
        the stubble grass
        along the wake
        of landbirds

& through the mysteries of dusk.

Come & going & standing still
I welcome them . . .

draw near. draw near. speak
or remain silent
        as you will .

3/
We have nothing to say
that will ever
unsay
what has been said
        for each shadow
        there is a source of light
        for each movement
        a beginning & an end

words but extend
the darkness & bend
the light

though mouths within
the crystal net of space

open & close
close & open

there is nothing new to be said
save

the universal mouth
betrays the head
& tediously so, withal

save realities come
&
strangers go

& that is all . . .

4/
The sick doctor &
the lawyer awaiting execution
lean a space on some pillared door

above them in blue
mosaic tiles
the frieze
            of life
                        explodes
in slow motion & silence

& on the horizon an awesome angel burns.

5/

machinery of war as beautiful
as absolute
as tedious
as death itself
glides past along the green canals
where old men shuffle in the stubbled dusk

while one , dressed in algebra
treads lightly in the plain . . .

this is no matter. great or small. hallucinations
come

&

travellers go. &
that is all.

all.

6/

in the pale evening
I am laid
in my own warm skin
beneath the giantess
of space

whose
blue desert
consumes us

delicately
tenderly

as her eyes
slowly open
making room
for the fountains
& the flowers
of our lips

for the gifts
of our greatest moments

saying with the voiceless
words of the flesh

Here are the strangers
our source of life

     admit them !
     admit them !

7/
In the pale of the evening
every evening
1000 suns are born
& stars like flowers
are sprung

within the blue giantess
whose eyes open slowly

making room for
the momentary flowers
& tender claws
& aching wings !

1000 suns are born
great & small
& in the distant impartial war

no travellers
no visitors
no strangers
fall.

The Orange Grove

(Valencia, 1962)

In idea, in sound, or in gesture the DUENDE likes
a straight fight with the creator on the edge of the well.
While angel, and muse are content with measured
rhythm, or the violin, the DUENDE wounds . . .
                    Lorca . . . ' The Theory and function
                                of the DUENDE '

I.

the long white wall
carves down the morning light
& multiplies the meagre sea

I sit
drinking cheap anís from out
a frosted glass
considering the passage of the blue
shadow
          & its significance . . .

the pewter beach holds no mystery.
squat children, far away, below the town
lisp
    to its speckled length
    crouching in its most
outflung fingers . . .

suddenly

from the shadow a young girl springs
walking with that unstudied poise
the virgin brings
to practised paths of harlots
before the lifesick eyes

of the guitar
                kings
& to those almond lusts of bitter boys
long dead beneath the masks of men . . .

whose blue birds sing in dreams alone
being of dry
                & custom weathered stone.

above the tables
from the high balconies & hot rooms
the voices cease
& it becomes so quiet
that I am aware of the clock

over dead water in its gaunt tower
winding up on fine springs
                            to strike
above the blue
& timeless guitar

the dark eleventh hour.

2.
out of darkness you have come
no angel or muse

wandering soulful
& alone

disguised as light
through labyrinths of self
as any maiden

seeking,
        seeking the orange groves
        of delight

I am not blind; nor lovestung
nor drunk

though all things wither
in the heat of day
& bells chime
& narrow streets deserted with that dread
of noon
echo, echo within the cells of time
recalling former harmonies of claw

& wing & flesh

or visions of love's truth !
No !

I am not blind—
though sprung from shadow

& born in war; Light ! I sing
& Blood !

& hold to no fixed law of seed
or stone
        or mysteries of youth !

out of darkness I have come
disguised as death

voyaging silent & alone
as any knight

beneath the blue guitar
& emblematic shadow of his house

my sullen lord! whose breath
moves quietly in the high

throat of noon
                as bells move too
                within the tower

encircling me with time
again

until the clock strikes up the hour
& I am faceless.

3.
you are not blind , nor drunk, nor free

I see you shake with dread
recognising through my mask
the living dead

& though you scream & tear
your cloth heart full

from out the dream & stop love's breath
you willingly prepare for this gay death . . .

& I, bemused with light,
come broken up
                from out still water
                & the town
                to where
                        you wait . . .

99

& stoop for whiteness
at your throat

& taste the shadow there.

& there . . . against a low stone wall
in violent shadow
& the company
of quiet, still lizards

we shall go

swooning deep in wounds of love
softly,
gently through the masks

of darkness & of light
within the orange groves of delight.

4.
' love is a rare liqueur in the vial of my soul '

' you call it love ? I doubt time's mastery
or that of flesh & mind would let it out

should it exist so . . . '
beneath our lord's guitar
or shadow of his face . . .
rather, then,
this instant
in this life . . .

' a vast and timeless flower
—the mask of grace '

Ah! lovely, wounded child
know now that blood is wild
& love as free as light!

where you lay down in other times
the nettles grow
& overhead the carrion claw
glides to and fro

though all things break at your soft moan
the shadow & its phantom lover
will not cease to go !

5.
within the shade
& underneath the clock

you sit as one bemused
hugging lean breasts

to a leaner face
                  & courting silence .

‘ wait not too well upon it maiden
  lest you own it soon . . . ’

for there is madness in the light of noon
& a humour in the countryside abroad

where you have wandered singing & alone
beside yourself with love
beneath his hands
& beneath his face
& come at last / great with relief
to this quiet place .

Love is not rare as you suppose
nor clad in black; nor sorrowing

where drops are spilt upon the amber earth
the ageing, sightless king (at his last breath)

discerns a death
amongst the leaves
where nettles & where hemlock grows

but being blest with that third eye
& lizard quiet upon the rock of self

i conjure up the rose.

4. Pipe Dreams in Ponsonby

kingseat / my song: 1969

' newspapers released late in '69
th names of those GIs principally
charged with th atrocities in th
vietnamese hamlet of my lai (song mi)
one of these was cpl. david mitchell
aged 29. '

under perse skies
she lies
' as a 3 year old '
huddled against th earth
for a measure of peace.

here
in this hamlet
atrocities occur / too
though all these child
women
    are sick
save her. SAVE HER!
my lie is no trick
I mean it with all
I know—

my song doesn't matter
but
you know my name.

th most ill, here
wear white
& drool

under evening rituals
of carefully planned

indulgence. this army's
at
   ease. though th hour
is late . . . &
th prince
knew something to be
rotten
in th state.

my fragile, danish lover
has flowered in our dung
but
now / has been broken
at last
       &
they have washed her
       &
they have watched her
       &
they have stripped her
of all she had
—these fine nurses !
whose
slender fingers twitch
from no shock greater
than some ' gun miserable '
curiosity . . . (it figures)
these pathetic
panderings / & dismal lies
under th banners of tenderness
—this sinister guise . . .
from girls whose brows
are electric clear
& whose sad eyes
(triggers)
       are

simply
      mad.

sprawled on th grass
my true love lies
exhausted & sane
&
I see th scars of antique guilt
crisscrossing th pale temples
as of old
ah ! roseate
ah ! roseate faces of love
where
th object is futile
th cure lies
      in the act /

electric joy !
electric joy !

    . . .

now
all soldiers, too
in my song / or my lie
may descend to th depths
& ape
    no green dolphin
each is as free
as ' th other '
&
it has happened since time was
&
it has happened last month
under stars of duty &
banners of war /

                        a simple massacre
                        of th innocent / so
what ?

th logic's at th most primæval
stage . . .
ah ! th difference is
I, who must learn to live in my lie
I, was stricken, having spent
my self
            in my song / my sullen rage
            . . .
            the difference was th corporal
            bore my name &
            he
                is my dull age.

now
all soldiers , too, in my song
& poets in my lie
may descend & devour th invisible
children
            of themselves
under stars of duty &
th simple justice of axiomatic lust . . .
&
there are no regressions like
the regressions of love
&
there is no kingdom easier to come by
than th dust.

here
in th best institution
available
everybody is mad

' save my exhausted lover '
whose
temples hold th scab
of th cure
(as of old)
whose throat is twitching
in her daze
with the faint pulse   of those
th world chooses to murder
day by day &

        constantly &

        she

too
is learning how to kill . . .
&
I,

   I am trying to wish no one ill
am smugly assured that I
have done what I can—
am asked to leave
by a truly , terrifying monster

th doktor !

whose skin is raw
as all aborted schemes of love
whose voice is cold
(as of old)
who argues without a flaw
whose tone is smooth & drye !
though

        he cannot look me

           in th eye.

          . . .

I take my leave / ' on parole '
learning t' roll
with th dumb punches
(how they fall
  how they fall !)
learning
to live with mai lai
(as must we all !)
&
under the tall questions of my child
somehow I justify / these 29 years
worshipping in th vein'd temples of self
hoping that love, love will come through
& recalling my song / & the innocent / &
th unborn (who may yet, make it , too)
until
(playing a counting game) th little girl
 / asks ' what's your number ? ' & I
consider my fame / perplexed / as th next
one
     as to where to lay th blame . . .
' holy zero ' / I say / ' th most private rank '—
but then
I recall my name. &

                y'know / she knows / my lie &
                y'know / she knows my song &
                you know my song / & you
                know my name . . .

                my name is david mitchell

ritual

(fr Anna)

at this time
        when some pale, christ dry heart
        shakes & gibbers on hr shoulder
        like some gone disease or bird
        or
        with burning nostalgia fr th slime
        or word
        pounds blindly at hr throat
        with time's sick foot

at this time
        in th close of this 29th year
        in th keep of this concrete room
        pruned into th dark veined muscle
        of yet, another new city
        I plough th fugitive head; good
          & deep
            & set th old phonograph
                a turning . . .

once again
        houses across th bay hang red
        & savage
        through a veil of thin sun . . .

once again
        dressed in vivaldi's rosethorn coat
        you whisper
        through th dust motes of my untenanted
        body
          th illusion of blood . . .

once again

        th tender; much bruised flowers
        of yr throat
        close with my younger, phantom face . . .

at this time

        having recalled you
        I own again
        th steep paths of youth
        &
        I turn
           from th music
                th dream
                th truth
        wishing, again, to weep
        as once I did
        the
           old
               organic lie / this new
         and bitter mouth of ' love '
        must keep.

at pakiri beach

(for adrienne)

here
I sing th green branch
th lost hymn
to earth's green blood
& sap
& slime
to hold back time . . .

let me here give praise & tongue
to your bright flesh & hair & bone
to mouth & nostril / salt & lime
to breast & belly & that cool line
from throat to thigh; to all yr mouths
& voices / winedeep / lovestung
to silken down beneath th sun / about
th nipple
& all along th length of supple spine . . .

so hold / time ! & let us stand
since we are naked &
th blood is up
stay your bitter hand !

& let me here give praise & tongue
to teeth & earlobe ; sigh & chime
of deepest wells of love ; to breasts
like bells; to distant cries within
th drifting head / awash with swan pain
to these soft, inland eyes, gone out
this day on tides of goat pleasure
under
          sensual capricorn . . .

&
flesh I sing; th heavy vine; th green
voice branching up through throat
& down through spine; as thick as starmilk
or that yoke of springtide lust caught high
within th ancient ring of sea
& bone & sky
like dawn's blood in th midnight eye . . .

so hold / time ! & let us stand
since we are naked &
th blood is up
stay your bitter hand !

& let me here give praise & tongue
to your bright flesh
within whose silent web this moment past
have sprung; pale seeds as clear & warm
as tears; to this white rainbow; come
with dawn
to where th song fades bird like
on th feathered stave & broken
spoke of light . . .
to where th song fades O but does not die
lark ringing down
a waste of sky
             to where we lie.

bone

(fr elsebeth)

when all this sensual night has died
& dried away along th mottled skin

remember how it was
when I came in

to your cold hall

bearing th blind bone
bearing th cup & ball
bearing th glass with
th myriad flaws . . .
&
dreaming of gold &
dreaming of flight
yet
    locking
            invisible doors.

when all th swollen tongues
& arrowed teeth &
crystal eyes & tangled hair
& all / else / that you have known
leap up
within yr pale blood hands
in some distorted ball
in some black dream !

remember how it was / of old
when out from in between yr blood
dark thighs
        my sweet seed

& yours & ours alone
leapt sweetly up & danced
& danced
      & danced . . .
            I hope she dances
still.

when all this sensual night has died
& dried away along th mottled skin
remember how it was / those summer days
when
we drew orange blinds across the world's
enormous room / beneath th will—
breaking at first th green
of flesh
        for love
but finding it had lied
& locked us in—

we learned to break
th dream / fr loss . . .

& all too soon / th spirit
which
        though still—
        though small—

remains in each of us
th finest bone of all .

lullaby / blazing house

(for sara)

child's painting ; devonport naval dockyards
harbour sunset ; tree ; man ; princess ; long
jet aeroplane ; blazing house ; angel ; etc.

hey, little chicken legs, how come you cry ?
red is a find / do not fear red
though mars shine baleful through this evening
sky . . .
       th gone sun / like old father time
will tell you / tomorrow
                tomorrow belongs
to no tradition you cannot create; hey . . .
red is not final / do not fear red
              red is a find / red
            is a fine
                  tomorrow

ah ! my pisces child ! I cannot snare th moon
though I have tried / throw you instead
a small & falling star . . .
let it be green / let it be blue
let yr first wish be for peace / also th others
too ; th other 2 . . . peace
& a quiet time to dream
(row gently down th stream.)

tomorrow/   th navy disbands & sailors dig pipis
tomorrow/   th airforce fails & well, ah; we teach
                them bomber flyboys how to walk . . .
tomorrow/   th army breaks up altogether & soldiers
                plant grass . . .
tomorrow/   th screaming captains are kind old kings
                again / & they remember how to talk . . .

tomorrow/   th mad butcher goes from our street
tomorrow/   each of th 4 black horses dies
tomorrow/   there will be born; th fabulous white
             unicorn !
tomorrow/   flowers spring up through steel & concrete
             & th dancing girl flies . . .

tomorrow/   NO HOUSES BURN ! / tomorrow there will be
             a feast ! & a journey ! / &
             a return . . .

red is not final / do not fear red / no; & black likewise.

                a last word / now
fr yr masters & princes
fr yr madames & fools
                a last word / now fr yr
teachers & strangers . . .
                you ! who throw switches
                will never ring changes !
                voluntary machines!

money / power / comfort / discipline / timetables / uniforms
                THESE ARE TH DANGERS !
& you are to be enlightened / by way of dreams . . .

ah ! my pisces child ! I cannot snare th moon
though I have tried / throw you instead
a small & falling star . . .
let it be green / let it be blue
let yr first wish be for peace / also th others
too ; th other 2 . . . peace
& a quiet time to dream
(row gently down th stream.)

dream on / dream
a silver dream
sally serene . . . (hush now) tomorrow / no body weeps
   . . . wind in th pines . . .
       a steamer's whistle . . .
            ah ! voyages
             voyages !

dream on / dream
a silver dream
       sally serene . . . (hush now) . . . she sleeps.

letting go / early & late

when you look up, daughter
& break morning's sun stone
& wall of old grief
broadcasting yr gold
& lovely seeds of hope
around th heart's dry suburb

time wasted in sleep
or lost in th dream
looms tall in yr song
as yr own , sweetest, dreams
in their weave
(their finest stuff / no fabric
  cd keep)

fare thee well / say I
go lightly over all
& as you leave—
step high
step high
        though love
        choke th eye.

thief
of my heart's attic cell
solace
& bell of these days
against th caul & blaze
of th furies I own—
feast or fast
take what you can
from th crazy, old man
but

honour th dove
honour th dove.

& cast up th eye
through this high morning's light
to th fire of this green day
though each new mask
break, too, on its last . . .
only this
I ask—
     step high with love
     & honour th dove.

go lightly / go well
sally serene
vulcan I am & sire have been
though
flawed in th commerce of love
& th dream . . .

sing/ where you may be bound
sing/ as free birds on th wing
sing/ beyond all practised grief
&
smile at th player's lies
smile at them all
save this—

     I leave you now
     no words of good
     or ill /
          only
     th heart's slow
     madrigal.

despite th cloth of joy I wear
& fool's bright cap
I am th ageing king
—go lightly as morning . . .

th seasons change
th hammers ring
&
from th north
th invaders sing . . .

go lightly
go well
     sally serene

though sun stone & time
tap morning's gold hope
& shatter th dream

& th towers burn
& th wheels turn.

george raft hat

coming home ' without my mind '
sunday. 9 a.m. through grafton
gulley & over ' that bridge '

past th electric mouths
of yawning kids
braces on th teeth
& sulphur on th tongue

past some lush / all over hung
&
crashed on a slatted bench
all
crumpled & embryonic
(hand between th thighs)
worldly wise ! history unfurled !
ah ! dead ! / to ' th fucking worlde ! '

coming 'home' without my mind
again
watching th stories & poems
th people make
passing along th kerb
against th railings of th day
& rantings
            of th dead—

light / shade / light / shade
' as if from world to world '

through that gulley like jimson
& weeds in th electric head
& sudden

flashes / too
from out th void
th unknown / yeah.

o zone . . . o trackless
tram !

yr shazam bolt of striped lightning
glows in my eye a long time
         —a long time

under heavy skies / cool disguise
of patterned power ! nietzsche
lies
   in th gutter . . . / i hear him sing
   ' buy you a diamon' ring
   my frien' '
       the end. /

streaks of bacon lie curled
on th thick willow pattern plate
through th river of some restaurant window
& above this / in cursive script
up high / 180° / th legend
   TODAY   SPECIAL

brings me to th knees . . . ah !
that's th line ! / since time began
fr all who were brought up t'eat th shit
' real pretty '
      that's th line / th holy village
      th sunken city ! (since time began)
   TODAY   SPECIAL
on th instalment plan.

outside the jewish cemetery / 2 lean
& graceful pakistanis stand
th woman & th man
& i
am watching them watching me
watching . . .

& i am watching them in their sleeveless
fair isle pullovers / fawn & blue
& they look through
th years—
as they

        discuss th ' mawgan dovid '
        on th gate

& then
there are these, persons, in th trolley bus
who are watching, too
early & late
O

yeah.

&
now a flight of sparrows weaves between us all
th time of day

TH TIME OF DAY

& th green bus
slides

quietly

away.

ancient chinese philosopher in th george raft hat
& carpet slippers, too
leans ' a space ' against some wall
in th sudden sun

looking starry eyed ! looking great !—
(with th elements) O looking benign
(though slightly undone)
in th same
   old
     way . . . & he

is turning, now, to face th new
motorway monuments
from out old clay.
    behind him
    a huge
& juicy nude pouts / in orange & green
like marilyn's death mask
truly beautiful! in th karangahape road strip joint
closed (fr business) all in th cool day

o largesse ! o $ signs within th purple eye
o history unfurled !
    ah. wisdom / like th scent
    of rain . . .
coming 'home' without my mind / again . . .
    ah ! visions
      visions

VISIONS OF TH CARDBOARD WORLD !

antique seaman

this blond sailor's lying in th street
wrestling with some angel
yet
she knows he's flying, too
above th stoned islands of her body
where
th cool winds carry all who drift
above th useless feet . . .
&
she is well lushed &
blocked; yet incomplete / waiting still
for him to cease
to wax up pale & sorrowing
& have done soon with his lament . . .

&
she is leaning ' a space ' / up against
th maori hamburger bar
chewing some weird ' reality ' gum
2000 years gone
beneath th distant whine of sirens
– – – seeing things AS THEY REALLY ARE !
cool & warm & bent &
murmuring & sensual
& indolent.

&
she knows th meek shoulder slips
under burdens of 'love' & 'wonder'
& ' astonishment '
& she knows her breasts are hard
against th tide
& th simple softness of her body
drifting, too, in this marvellous year

is engulfed in time; yet will wear no fear
& she
(some sweet time before th dawn)
will help unwind th sheet
from off his ultimate form . . .
&
she will smile her damson smile
& he'll come through
to plumb th deepest sounds of love
anew.

        though angel / though tohunga burn
        & waltz time images of herself
        she never even knew she owned
        turn on her, too, within her turn
        until she knows & owns th ache
        ' can this be love ' / admitting
        then, that she may never see
        again
            th private rainbow break.

& he will smile his damson smile
& she'll come through
from out th hanging blue
to sound th deeps of love a while . . .
they will come through
they will come through

she's 16 / exquisite / a tremble
at th lip
&
on her skinny (lovely) arm
there is this blue tattoo—
a snake
a bird

a sailing ship.

th oldest game

below th house a rusty plateau
of ponsonby rooftops & chimneypots
like paris recalls other mountains
& other tents
                  & voyages. voyages.

here
above the fine & foreign flesh
of this strange SO familiar girl
he makes th signs . . .

&
her silken stomach rises
at the first & least touch
to his cold fingertips
&
her pale eyes close
against his lips . . .

& so intrudes th dream / th game / th trip
& yet she catches / still
beneath th felt breath turning
in th blue of memory
the tongues unspoken & unspelt
of how ' it used to be '
&
once again he asks (in silence) the same
old question
' what has this world done to us ? '
& she
replies / likewise / beneath th sightless eyes
' what have you done / lover
what have you done to me ? '

some compromise
some crutch of voiceless logic may spring up
for this sad pair
who learned to take / & not to care
& want too much / from out ' thin air '

they're walking th wire
  —walking th wire—
on one hand looms th fell abyss
on th other this crass world's
synthesis
        & in between /
                    th fire

its so very apt / then
that there should come th sound of seagulls
through th bright morning

& he's lying back there thinking
' what sad bells & death knocks their long throats are ! '

its so very apt / then
that th poppies in th vase are knocking too

& she's lying back there thinking
' those grave & oval blooms / how sad
& dry
    they knock together like ' serious heads '
    & close & die
    & close & die '

now
while her soft mouth brushes his own
& his hand dusts over her golden thigh
& th sun steadily rises over roofs
& chimneypots

like a gong of death
in th pewter sky . . .

she

fabricates hr little / lost moan / & he
groans to hear it
                    &

out from th cage of hr body
& his own
            lost & lovely / on memories blown
            on these
            &
            on dreams alone . . .

insubstantial lovebirds fly
& the gulls cry
& the gulls cry.

my lai / remuera / ponsonby

she
holds th mirror to her eye

whole villages burn

2 million years have proved nothing
she

did not already know.

th lines on hr hand
speak out clear   &

serene

also those beneath her eyes
& in between . . .

she
sits in th kitchen
' boiling an egg '

she
inverts th tiny
' hourglass '   &

30 seconds pass   &

she
contemplates th sand

                                              &

she
holds a hand over each dark eye
in turn
                                         &

children burn

ponsonby / remuera / my lai

th warrior's come home
there he goes !
right
      here
          & now

up queen street
in a gun carrier

palm to th clear brow
in th oldest, most obscene
salute
     & in th eyes
th mandrake root—

th blackened bone.

2 million years
have proved nothing
he did not already know
ah ! there he goes !

th kiwi's come home.

he
sits in th barber's chair
' short back & sides '
& he
lingers in th chemist
buying coloured slides
& he
ponders on time / yeah. &
destiny; /

         also th fates . . .
& he
sits in th kitchen
playing poker with his mates
& he
contemplates his hand
& he
holds a king
          to each soft lip
in turn

& th others pass
(& he waits his turn)

& 30 seconds pass
& he
    plays his hand

&

    children burn.

harlequin at home

& he has marvelled at the clear bright voice of time
within th sheltered chapel of its tree
sold hours scarcely weaned
with hesitation born of death's sure gong or tic
of sudden life
like some young cousin to th hawk; in his moist earth
he cowers t'watch th world go by
in this hemisphere's best /
                      bombing weather / O masters
he sing fr you !

& he has dwelt in fear upon th stations of yr war
& jigg'd th wordless dance & gagged upon yr gallow
gibbet swollen at th tortured tongue & cloven in th shallow
stance of sleep; (th jester's life t'keep) with one eye
open only; saw he meet / t'keep th silence ! as do fit th foole !
in this crass companie where silence is th rule . . .
& he
has turned th lifesick eyes at last
above th glass; above th sullen leaves of th savage promise
pocketed th fell currency with trembling hands
alive only to th debts they owne / before th tomb
its darkest treaty ! / O masters, true, he sings
fr you !

& he has tried to own th self ; at least within th steady tick
& chime of th sinister going ; running out & looking in
to that brute cage of flesh ; fr dignity at last
who first sandblasted with th grains of time ; th oldest war
is sprung no more against th general heart; or at th yoke
of th whitened bone's ellipse; who falls at last
collapsing with th weight of blood on other's hands
then views his own ! & shakes / & wrings them then

in stupid pain; above th raw meat & th guilt & blame
whereon th carrion flies of time do drink their lust
whereon th rain is hot & pink; & sacrosanct again
whereon th dream is down (beneath th dust); th mind is blown
& napalm feeds th brain . . . O masters, masters, he sings
fr you !
& he is sick; yr sometime boy, who was th green & dancing stick
th sometime joker's blind with pain: waiting on th screaming
captains & th envoys in th base campaign , to cease; or turn
& come again . . . & he
has marvelled; still; th clear bright signs
that visit with th steady voice their own dread stealth
& omen truth; (th twins of time & pain) against th dreamers
& th dream ; of love ; of peace ; of youth . . .
like ancient music a turning & a turning in th blue / ah !

      th lay is sullen / yet th song is true
          & he is singing yet
            despite
      those keenest knives ' & few ' / th
      raising of th voice contrives . . .
O master; masters; masters; true ! / he sings fr you !

         THERE IS NO INNOCENCE FR HE
      WHO PONDERS TIME &
    BLOOD &
CLEMENCY
THOUGH
     DREAMS
        RISE UP LIKE HARMONY
        WHERE BEES ONCE WERE & HONEY GREW . . .

yr midnight mass beneath th sword
is over & th spirit's through
bastards
       of th sometime true
       he sings fr you . . .

       th mongrel under th board.

th yes sheet

TITLE	:	NATURE OF COMMUNICATION
SUBTITLE	:	COMMUNICATION OF NATURE
PURPOSE	:	PROPAGANDA
TOPIC	:	NATURE OF TH UNIVERSE
MESSAGE	:	LOVE
VEHICLE	:	FLESH
SEASON	:	SPRING
YEAR	:	NINETEEN SEVENTY ONE
TIME	:	SIX THIRTY SEVEN A.M.
DAY	:	SUNDAY
LOCATION	:	BED
PROPS	:	GREEN BRANCH / BUDS / OPEN SHUTTERS / ETC.
PERSONNEL	:	SELF WOMAN MUSE ANGEL / & ANCESTORS (VARIOUS)
ZODIAC.REF	:	CAPRICORN / LEO / EXL.MARK / REPEAT EXL.MARK.
STATION	:	NATURAL HIGH
TECH.LABEL	:	POEM
PERS.LABEL	:	MITCHELL D
STATEMENT	:	CONSISTENT AFFIRMATIVE / REPEAT / AFFIRMATIVE
LYRIC	:	

yes

/ cont

laughing with th taniwha

if I am sitting motionless
at yet another blue window
of early evening

please do not think
neighbour

that th dream is one of grief
for this
& other days;   after all
there have been so many worlds
between th bell & th blue star !
no . . .
th sad year is out / th river
th pool is clear !

& th monstrous claws of time
no longer scar this life . . .

there have been others / near
& far

there have been worse / I own
& you'll agree
sitting on th step
& smoking th pipe . . .

listening to mozart / like
in some european village
of th previous soul. also

some jelly roll / yeah. & th
sitar / too

beneath th blue.

occasionally you look up at me
as if wondering at this evening
habit of mine . . .

time is no more th death heavy creek
nor bitter end . . . no . . . friend

I do not wish to wish upon some holy star
all stars are holy ! all skies are blue !
neighbour / I love mozart / & th sitar, too
also, neighbour . . . / think . . .
I love you !

I do not wish to wish upon some holy star
I'm just waking up / to myself /
about time !

yeah
        & laughing with th taniwha

mad dog errol

here he come !
mad dog errol
hey
    hey
        foamy lip
smiley mouth
what
    teeth
        bite
you ?
    &
who
    drive you
round
&
round
&
round ? & who
broke yr hip
&
cool ? & what
now DO you say
in your weird way ?
hey
    hey
        stumble toe
how come you limp
& O so scratchy go ?

shit eater !
system beater !
aye / aii / ayii !
slinky eye

141

little
    brittle
        pinky
prick
hey
    hey
        hey
            what now
DO you say
in your weird way ?

here he come / there he go
& ah. hell. no. he aint
sick
    (just a little people
shy)
    & th tail up high
        & one eye on th sky . . .

there he goes / follow his nose
& he don't ask why . . .

mad dog errol
hey
    hey
        hey
next time round
you'll be ok . . .

windfall

th oranges in th bowl
really belong
to ward 7.

th nurse / however / has
brought them in here
' fr th children '

they don't amount to much
small, bruised fruit, still
there they are
          on th window sill . . .
familiar suns
against th willow pattern
dark blue & ice
& th ' sensuous rill ' ah !
some kind of paradise.

th oranges in th bowl
are / undeniably / larger
than life
          to maureen fiona
                    chantal . . .
yeah.
well, she's 4 / nearly 5
still
glad to be alive / &

lucky.

          1 broken arm
          3 broken ribs
          fractured skull
          & massive shock . . . yeah. &

she
has lain there   2 weeks
beneath this world's crass clock
in th bruised pits of ' reality '
feeling / ' a bit cold '
watching th dust motes dance
in th early sun (as of old)
& considering th gold cheeks
of th oranges . . .
she's lying there / alone / discreetly
watching th sun make time
with its own (as of old) & sweetly !
&
sweetly.

tomorrow th aliens come
th woman & th man
tomorrow is th birthday
(she's forgotten th other, darker anniversary)
tomorrow there will be gifts in th nursery
– – – according to th plan; yeah. looks
' of love ' / & story books / with th pictures above
a doll

        an apple / maybe / & a ginger
        bread man . . . yeah. & voices; voices; voices
        from some star . . .
        (she's forgotten whose they are)

potato chips ? licorice, darling ?
    a

        mars

            bar ?

aesthetics

that harlequin / he's sure
some liar

he sd t' me
TH SHIPS ON FIRE !

i strate way leap
into th ocean

& there i freak
out in slow
motion

th ship sail on
across th sea

& leave this
' darkling werlde '

t'me . . .

now th sun go over
th horizon

but i cn see
th pale moon

rising

& th mermaids come
& sing real pretty

from out some sweet
deep

groovy city . . .

yeah.

i lie back coole
& easy float

i do not really miss th boat.

words

who
seeks wisdom in words

seeks best &
first
        th signs
below their bland faces
&

between th lines . . .

who
faces silence in fear

best
shout & dance & sing
some
        song . . .

all night long
&
year
        after
                year.

5. Myths of Woolloomooloo

yellow room

he is sitting in the café lebanon
& his legs are crossed beneath th balls
& th traffic in the street is slow . . .
&
he is waiting, while he is sitting in th café lebanon
fr something GREAT to happen . . .
&
her face, in th mirror on th wall
reflects her boredom . . .
&
his face, is in th mirror, too
looking ' deep '

but all he's thinking is :
' that waitress is asleep '
&
there comes a curious palpitation in th traffic
& th green bus goes by. there it goes !
                    (it has gone)
&
his balls ache
while he is sitting in th café lebanon
waiting fr something GREAT to happen
(his balls are waiting, too)
yet
he cannot bring himself to uncross his legs—
his balls . . .
&
he is smoking
while he is sitting in th café lebanon
waiting fr something GREAT to happen

. . .

now
outside th traffic has jammed up ; stopped
completely
&
his cigarette burns down ; goes out
&
she scratches her wrist; absent minded
glazed eyes gone yellow with winter
&
now, she is scratching with th other hand
& outside th bus driver cuts his idling engine
&
they are still
          sitting in the café lebanon
waiting for something GREAT to happen

&
that seems to be all—

o yeah.

&

A FINE RAIN BEGINS T'FALL.

A small sincere poem for Davnet

Fog horns

break
through—

to where
under the small

ornate windows
of time

you sway

as if
already lost.

Willows
too sway—

I am
the broken branch

I see you
smile

&, I
half tremble

yes—

like
a strong reed

in the lakes

of
the flesh.

old song

upstairs
the guests are rising
from the long table . . .

voices drift
as if across the years

there comes
the scraping of the chairs
the brittle whisper
of the wineglasses
the muted shriek
of a child; the mild
roar
of an old man
&   laughter
        laughter

like iced water
in a stone jar . . .

the host shrugs
& turns up the eye
as if to say
(with a sigh)

' they are as they are '

voices drift
for an instant
along the staves
of afternoon
lightly
lightly

all in the gathering blue

. . . its a snatch of old song
        comes drifting through . . .

myth has it
the old lady woke at 4 p.m.
' is it the revolution ? '
she wanted to know . . .
(' soon / madam / soon
 it wont be long ')

the maid served pernod.

upstairs
the guests are rising
from the long table . . .

clarinet, fiddle
soprano

bassoon . . .

' come nellie / come
        hannah
 come sasha
 come june

a little piece for the visit
& the rising of the moon ! '

outside
in the geometric shade
beneath the bare vine of winter

the apprenticed lute
he
sits alone

honing the blade
honing the blade

all in the gathering blue

. . . its a snatch of old song
   comes drifting through . . .

myth has it
the old man woke at 6 p.m.
' what news / what news
  from the coast ? '

(soon / master / soon
  . . . it wont be long)

they gathered round
they drank a toast

' here's to you / &
  here's to you / &

  here's to you ! '

upstairs
the guests are seated
at the long table . . .

soon

they rise again

there comes
the scraping of the chairs
the small voices of the glass
& the gentle mirth
of the girls
& the players
& the children
& the old men

& laughter
    laughter

' for all its worth '

above the scent of the rain
beneath a sickle moon
all in
        the gathering blue

ah . . . its a snatch of old song
        comes drifting through . . .

now
the lamps are lit

its
growing late

& dark

now
the horseman's at the gate

&
the prussian hound

he
hugs the earth

he
does not bark

he

makes

no

sound . . .

diana

th golden girl
is buying apples

she
moves down th street
with
astounding grace

th green iris
of th harbour
opens
to receive her . . .

th winter sun
is th last
cool oracle
she needs . . .

its gentle glow
lights up her
face.

inside th persian
carpet stall
3 very wise men
are discussing
cut price warfare
& flights to europe

they fall
silent as she passes
then they lean
against th white wall.

across th street
th newsboy's son

he's chewing licorice
he's folding little
purple darts
from waxed paper
&
he's throwing them
at her feet /
              & he's singing !

' helios !
  helios ! '

at dusk

at dusk
the stars drift in

at dusk
krishna

dances with the cowgirl

at dusk the valkyries ride out
& ulysses comes home

calliope
terpsichore

the devout
the flickering lamps

of this ordinary street
betray the lust for gods

in every man

presage the carnage
& sanctify the dust

of history

& history . . .
history's a rolling

trackless tram
& tomorrow's ozone

she is my winter love
the season kills

all pleasure proves

she stirs beneath me
& the mountain moves

& while the heart moves gently
& while the flesh lies

on the bone
there's no great truth

i will condone
like love

& love
& love alone

melba hooks

(for dame nellie melba)

love's the blue destiny
her arms reached out for

along the picket lines
of woolloomooloo

& st petersburg

along the barricades
of circumstance

lost found lost
forever

along the savage ether
along the blue radio waves

rippling like chords of hair
down some pale temple

of the static revolution

down the long
hallways of the dream

lost found lost

like this boeing
in its progress

like this coastline
through pale cloud

like those blue lips
of old wounds

one is always sure
to recognise

in the weird architecture
of the cumulus

rainbanks

in the bizarre, familiar design
of certain radio dials

circa 1931

the tattered
banners of love

from out old paintings

like absinthe
like pernod

like spanish fly
like the quiet

ecstasy

of the saints
in days of old

like the quiet
ecstasy

of executioners
in days of old

like the adolescent voices
of french horns

along the savage ether

like fog burnishing
antique chests

in portobello road

like these sad plaster
child women

who reach out reach out

from all apertures
of the dream

from st vincent de paul
gloom temples

goosed
only on the 2nd hand figures

of water clocks
roman chimes

hourglass heroines
do you long do you long

these sad girls who wait
only to stop waiting

for what blue destiny
do you long

blue lips
blue temples of love

of song

to split again

(the fair smile of mother earth)

3 men
baling hay

a hawk
over brown hills
like
some remembered
hand
        over
the fair smile
of mother earth

a hawk
over brown hills
&
along the metalled
road

lorikeets
&
magpies

staging their quaint
little parliament

calling   ' India !
       India ! '

ah . . . the politics
      th politics

confound !

& I

am sitting still
in Queensland

watching the ancient
shadow play

of earth
& hawk &

3 men
baling hay.

compulsory stop

now
here's th mystery !

he's standing at th compulsory
stop
with th crippled lady
&
he's toying with her crutch
&
he's reading aloud from some
colonial history

sincerely, sincerely !
like it ws some

holy creed
          / its th mystery
              th mystery!

cd be some prophet
cd be some
visionary
          like
albion's seed
cd be a poodle
on a lead
          / but it aint
. . . its just another poet's
  forgotten how t' bleed

i have t'tell him
th heart of these facts

ws once blown with song
he sd
botany bay's where you belong . . .

i have t'tell him
dead
things rot & stink
he sd
come over the LEAGUES
i need a drink . . .

i have t'tell him i think
he's wasting precious time
he sd—
its mine ! someone has
t'chart these fatigues . . .

he's sweating like th bridge
he wants t'be
under th horsemen !
                              / friend
what we need is a poem
that feeds itself
& leaves you starving / its there !

its in th rime ! & next week
like always
may yet be / th holy time !

ok / so the poet's AT HOME
there he is !

sitting under th tassled lampshade
chasing the acapulco moths
of gold
bending th same old dumb

circles
th times have made

beneath th parasols of bone

he's quite alone
though
this

is

something he
will never quite condone.

regulations require that he fast
(he cant)

particular attention shd be paid
to th denim

werkshirt
&
th stubbled chin: note also
th heavy frown—

this denotes he's busy
yeah.
taking himself in
&
putting himself down

ok / so th poet's AT HOME
i seen him at it last night
sitting in th convict stone
room
at th deal table

one glass only before him
red wine /
                    ws it burgundy?

ok / enough
th times are out of joint
& so is he /
                    its rough . . .

but on th floor th cigarette
packet bears th legend

    GITANES

yeah. gypsies. & on th box
of his werlde / too / there is
this dark lady
                    dancing . . .

don't ask who / cs he aint sure
who'll climb in th window
who'll break down th door . . .

/ friend
            its only just begun
            its only just begun

        &

            that's how it is done
            under th sun

cd be some romantick
indulging th deepest
need
cd be some prophet

pushing his strange
seed
cd be a poodle
on th plastick
lead . . .
but it aint /

    its just another poet
    studying t' bleed

stone blue chain

to seat himself before th fire
vulcan had t'bend
now
its th forge that's bent
&
over in th far corner
th limping smith
drags chains
of gold

like excrement . . .

waiting for th law
waiting fr some
stone
          tablet
t'bend /
          waiting to stop
          waiting . . .

th warden sd
' in here you get used to
th life . . .
          it gets you in th
          end. '

waiting fr th word
waiting fr th traveller
from ' other lands '
waiting fr th falling
siren or star
seeing in th cool eye
of his mind

th greek pigeon
leaning on th bar

yeah

& up in darlinghurst
in every paper

th sombre politicians
of love

are murmuring ' he's one
of us . . . '

as if th fancy denim
suits cd hide th pus

yeah. & willie mac th dove
& smilin' jack th kiwi glove

they go ' werking class '
each to his own

working brass between th teeth
fr LOVE
           & leather in th hands . . .

there's yr myths of woolloomooloo
the blind fold / th brass & gold

& th stone blue chain
about th bone / again
                  & again

                  & again.

bewdie resists time's deluge

(at nimbin n.s.w.)

coming

by slow degrees
through

ancient texts
like jewelsa

social realism
darl . . .

across the
the complexities

of yr face . . .

coming

at last
to this

watershed of hope
like adolescent

bravura

against th flode
of time !

coming

on twisted
high ways

of love

like lawson, angular
in late afternoon light

on the platform
of vulture street

station / cityside
not

river side

coming

down myself
i now decide

to set down
as carelessly

as truth permits

the husk & word &
seed

that may no longer
be denied

' where rivers lie
still
against the tide
the sea's truth
comes home

                    this
no heart
may hide '

it is dusk
day is going

fast
        / now
nellie's in
the billiard

saloon

she's quite alone
seems like love's

the blue
destiny her slender

arms reach out for

& just
now
        / the rising
        of the moon

on brisbane waters
on brisbane waters

& on the jukebox
' across th great divide '

&

' down along the riverside '

176

like these shades of love
      gone by
            gone by . . .

these apparitions

/ like lawson, angular
      like nellie
            alone . . .

cd be listening
for th telephone

or, for the storm
warning

on the abc wireless
cd be

their hats , upturned
expecting rain

cd be a waiting, jes
a waiting

for a train . . .

like love, love love
& the angel bone

faces of calliope's
daughters
&
just now

the rising of the moon
on brisbane waters

like henry, angular
like melba alone

but

then, love
is love is love / another

matter

or so they say

at surfer's &
in coolangatta

th good moment

he came in as if out of the rain
to the dry flickering warmth
of her smile

she was a refuge
he was the stranger

they threw memories
dreams on the fire

like driftwood

until th good moment
glowed . . .

i would that all such
chance meeting

were as sweet.

a futile hope to judge
from that deep grief

& violence i see

in faces on the coloured screen
on faces in the street . . .

she went out as if into the bright day
leaving   the dream

for him to bury
& to mourn.

he was the husbandman
stoop'd

on the sunslope
tending the black vine
drinking the hard wine

till the sun
struck him silly

& he began to sow
broadcasting hope

the long afternoon
through . . .

cool air
queensland clouds

banked
purple as wine

a sudden dusk
soft rain

cold night air
moving in the pines

beyond
the circle of the light

—evening's cold dues
lady /

wherever you are
heed this

& walk easy—

you walk
with the muse.

6. Dark Fire

the poetry reading

the girl at the window
is gazing out to sea

monsieur
has just

taken off
his camelhair coat

the maid is wasting time
at the mirror

monsieur
lights a cigar

madame engages
a friend

in conversation

footsteps on the
stair

like small alarms
precede the welcome

which must surely
follow

the new guests
taking off their

camelhair coats
wasting time

at the mirror
lighting cigars

engaging friends
in conversation

fabricating small alarms
for the pale girl

at the window
who is gazing

on the sea.

chess

these tall women
who

have just come
from mass

dressed in black
black
black

&

these pale men
who

have just come
from mass

dressed in black
black
black

do
not pause
to consider
the plaster eyes
eyes
of
the virgin . . .

nor the bilious
eyes
of

the
beggar
in the square . . .

nor
the indolent
eyes
of the children
on the footpath . . .

nor
the crafty eyes
of the street artist
in his progress . . .

nor
the doleful eyes
of the poodle
on his lead . . .

they
are blind

these 6
peasants

&

are led
slowly

to a white
white

white
taxi

/ one
by
one

by
one

very serious
very

young

nun .

olive grove / noon

(for garcia lorca)

deliver me
olive tree

from my hard silence

an old woman carries fruit
an old dog crosses the square
diagonally

the wind blows

deliver me   o   sacred tree
from the eye of the storm

my houses are razed
my armies imaginary

my ladies are ghosts
my friends

enemies

my gardens are devoured
by the sea

my times are treacherous
my dreams, cowards

they turn
they turn

& flee

deliver me   o   sacred tree
from my hard silence.

an old man carries himself
across the square

in agony

the times are treacherous
his brothers have seen
to that

they are dead
his brothers

still he carries them
across this square

they are my brothers
deliver them   o   sacred tree

from their hard silence
o   sacred tree

an old woman carries flowers
she crosses the square

silently , silently .

the keening

cypresses above the tombs
lean together

conspire
like brothers , like sisters

like dancers
like trees

against the faultless
shell

of the sky . . .

their shadows
on a white marble frieze

cyphers

wrought beneath a sun
full blown

with that golden rose of noon
& noon's slow

bells, bells &
pigeons

flung
against the crumpled

curtains of the sea
they soar , they fall , they soar

their shadows
on that bright element

are clawmarks on the pale daymoon
shadows on the tent of life

or cyphers on a tomb—bells
bells & something more

an alien sound
i had not heard before

the day
goes ahead

a child comes with bread

the arc of his arm

as he broadcasts
the crumbs

turning deep
from within the arc of his eye

& out

to that greater arc
where pigeons

fly

are flung across this satin drop
whereon the verie early stars are hung

& so
& so

the mime; the bells; the word
this desart rosarie

this turquoise bridge
between a jungle &

a lord.

th persistence of poesie

(for J. L. Borges)

was a king
had 7 birds

they got
away

he never
died

just disappeared

all in
the heat

of the day

one moment stood
before a wall

of granite &
of masonry

one moment
stood

before his time
the next

eternity . . .

the ages passed
the ages rolled

beneath the sky

came 7 birds
to seek a king

electing each
a note to sing

to break
the glass

of time ; to rend
the cage
  / each
of his age

or to spread his
wings
& fly . . .

the ages passed
the ages rolled

beneath the sky

7 birds before a wall
reflected in a blind man's eye.

a mild summer's air

mademoiselle
your presence

in this room
changes the sun

in its course

already, already
the tulips

are wilting in the vase

see ! now the cypress
in the window

is playing shadow games
behind your golden hair

who bottles time ? or the sun
or the mysteries behind

your eyes?

the wine betrays itself
bacchus sulks

in a corner
his customary lair

ah! let him stay there !
& mars—dissipated on

this mild summer's air—
let them envy us

your eyes enticing the cypress
the tulips the sea

my poet's mouth
quite bare

of charms or words

let them envy us this &
onlie this—

one

sweet

kiss.

sentinel

orange grove
olive grove

mountains &
sea . . .

through these trees i see
the ancient navies

the lines of gold
warriors

dark against the blue

the magic eye
on the prow of each ship

hypnotising the coast
with an alien power

through these rock formations
i see

the painted hulls
the painted sails

that crowd the sea
encircling the heroes
&
waiting on the land which, also
serves . . .

through these boughs i see
the children of the innocent

making jaded, pauper preparation
for war

through these fell historic leaves , i see
the rough hewn tree!
the limbs of bloodied grief !
the murdered leaves of glorie !
the scarlet, blackened, blistered thief !

through these words i see, the true theatre of war
the human heart

then off damned succubus . . . sloth !
O absalom ! O astaroth !

now, into this arena
poised & eloquent

the silence of a land bird's flight
has also fallen / like gift / like a wish

so now, the peace
the balance

the equipoise &
the poem

mohamet's scimitar
simurg's seven birds
yahweh's wrath

christ the fish.

blackamoors

the sea
ignoring the day

moon
disappears

into
africa

i hear a jackal
laugh

i hear the drums
of the black

millionaires
those who have

nothing
but clean air

to breathe &
a proud spirit

pulled by the
politics

of the winds
into

crumbling europe

i see their sons
& daughters

silent as stone
in the streets

i hear the rustle
of 500 franc notes

in their voices
they speak money

they do not praise it
they eat

money
they do not worship

it. for this i, at least
honour them.

rimbaud

poets were looked on
as prophets
in his country . . .
he left.

he went
everywhere
with a rare good will

seeking a prophet.

every lousy city
he passed through
had its poets

& its lice . . .

he sold his poets licence
fr a schooner

fell in love with th sea

fell in the sea

went mad

loved his madness
perhaps a little
too much . . .

came back ' home '
—a nice touch

to die.

with rare good will
he is remembered by his country

as a much travelled stone

now
permanently set

in th firmament . his loss
ws a sad one

naturally
it came to pass

poets leaned

at the graveside
looking on

fr profit . . .

one
his head in the stars
sd /
        ' yes illumination
        this is what he meant . . . '

        & naturally
          naturally—it came to pass

        the dark clouds rolled
        down on charleville &

        on clichy &
        on montparnasse.

demi mondaine

you should have been born
in a temple

you should have understood
your natural affinity

for stone knives
for bells
for incense

for the commerce
of dreams

was holy . . .

as it is
the ground

beneath your
feet

still

claims your
rare

astonishment
your

occasional
wonder

the shrug
of yr slim

shoulders
in the rain

        / this
nonchalance

mademoiselle !
as if yr head

were, truly, in
the stars . . .

here
in this drab
seaport

in its oubliettes
& bars
you make boredom yr miracle
& silence yr pain

as if you did not know
they are painting you

painting you

these rough artists
these lords you serve

& never see again
these priests

you nevertheless
blindfold & chain

these hungry brothers
you do not feed in vain.

liberty

take up a stick
find suitable stones

a little cement
& some water

break the earth

feed it, brother &
it will feed you !

philosophers
will tell you all

you wish to know
of this prison

you are about
to build . . .

might as well save time
& finally accept

the logic
of seabirds

the charm &
formality

of dusk.

perhaps
sometime there

on the silence
of the universe

you will want
to hang

a few
notes . . . nothing

wrong
with that !

music's the magic
against the abyss

& wild beasts &
    the abyss

is a wild beast. go
ahead

no more honourable task
ever claimed

a man's evening. a song
is an eternity

even a poor song
ahem

especially a poor song

like the drone
of the driftwood & th pebbles

like the harmonies that are not
in this poem

like the friends who
do not sit in yr houses

but are there , nevertheless
like the sea

like the mouths of the sea
like the winds

& philosophers & you & me

chained like wild beasts
in this poem

yes. the one i now persuade
myself is coming to an end

the one i am about to call

liberty.

van gogh

the iron bells toll
the train pulls in

the evening carries
birdsong

gracefully

against the pines
& cypresses

& on the distant scroll
of the sea

madame comes from the gloom

she bears a little flag

she cuts the twilight
with her arm

her flag

she
is doing her duty

it is pleasing to see

her uniform is blue against the varnished sleepers

along the narrow platform
the pullman passengers are making haste

vincent appears carrying a cardboard suit
case

he looks a little ill
at ease

he doesn't look like he's got much time to waste
beyond the mediterranean angle

of his left shoulder
the stars are falling &

climbing
& going to waste

as is their wont

some are blazing it seems far too brazenly
some waver & dip at the rim at the rim

of the sea

some tumble & roll
                    it seems aimlessly
                                aimlessly

like an unwritten law
like a yacht that will

not come about
the train pulls out

the footsteps fade
the white waves roll

the dark bells toll.

soror mystica

now i leave
her

tenderly

&

tenderly
i go

from the bed
to the mirror

to the bathroom
to the hall

to the street

to the métro
to the night

to the place contrescarpe
to the pont neuf
to the black waters
of oblivion

to the void of sleep
& sleep

& sleep & tomorrow &
            tomorrow
                        &

tomorrow &
to boredom &
to ecstasie &

to death

& to literature & to all
the other diseases
that plague the fallen
fallen
       fallen
           condition of

                man . . .

& to walk humid streets
in continents
that spread out before me
like women
&
to freeze in the past
& to haunt unknown friends
of the future / already

& to pine in the present &
in the present to burn !

i walk the brute river
all things to unlearn !

save

one tender woman
    to whom

    in my dreams
      i'll always

        return.

Dark Fire

i see the leaders long gone & those who did not lead
on th wheels of good fortune
come back; come back begging forgiveness
from the street singers & dancers & fooles
from the street artists & poets & gypsies & bourgeois christian stools
three legged in th dog star night; undone; wailing
on freedom freedom ; i meet them i see them
their eyes wine bright with a lost desire
their bodies twisted like bread
they blaze
they blaze in the dream's dark fire . . .

i see th warrior chieftains & th cowards in camp array
sunder'd on the awesome age; come back come through
seeking forgiveness from th bards th children & th aged
who do not forgive them; who are too proud & blind
& wilful & stoned to see them; to forgive them
to teach them again that all things burn
that all things return ; i see them ! buckled on th faggots
of commerce; religion; intrigue; philosophy; to teach me
what i must needs learn; that man is chain'd that man is free

it is not their groans their shrieks their agony
from which i learn
it is the silences ; silences
behind each
in turn
perhaps it is the laws of chance
of serendipity / that shew t'me
the leaders long lost & those who did not lead
on th wheels of good fortune—they
that spring from th leaves of old bokes; interrogations
proclamations

their bodies twisted like bread
their eyes wine bright with a gone desire
they that blaze
blaze blaze in the dream's dark fire . . .

who is it dreams me? / who dreams us all?
who stands beyond the sundials
                    the fountains

                    mocking
                    mocking
as the mountain's silence mocks the plain
as the silence of the plain
mocks
            the questions of the sea

who dreams for you? who dreams
for me?

between these ' alpes maritimes '
& the lowlands sea
between Afric's sullen strand

                                    & pharaoh's land
                                    & tennessee

between rome's bronze dugs
& the hills of home
& thessaloniki ?

between newsweek magazine &
time magazine & the colour tv ?

between buddha's brass peace
& david's tomb
& bourgeois
christianity ?

who do i dream as all things fall
& who is it dreams for me ?

who dreams for us all ?

. . .

françoise brings cut flowers
they lie like children in the sun

she places them in water
the vase gives back
their bloom

they are heroes, dancers
each one

she goes so quietly
through this room

this place / departing . . .
                    returning . . .

the sun gives itself freely
through her hair

her eyes are on holiday
from paris

is paris at work ? o is paris burning ?

we meet on the wheels
of good fortune
                    / good grace

her body is dripping with salt water
her lips follow the birdsong
of afternoon /
                        of gold, of blue—
her mouth is an honest liar
from the ramparts of montmartre
from the fields of burgundy
from modest emotion / & from souvenirs, souvenirs . . .
like le mururoa & l'indochine & l'algerie . . .

she looks like io, but is persephone

her mouth is my mouth / il mentent vérité !

alors ! françoise, daughter of france
vive la liberté ; & on
with the dance

and . . .

are we not

damned & judged
& slaughtered & broken

& silent & innocent
& alone
            together . . .

explosions from
the cliffs
trace . . . birdsong &
afternoon / . . .

her hand like
silence

on the quarry
of my face . . .

flowers cut
while in full

bloom . . .

& words . . .

& words that wither
in a sunlit room

. . .

who does she dream ?
who walks beyond
the twisted future
in her hair

her afternoons

shadows on a whitewashed wall
a brightness in the air

her mouth at my shoulder
its dumb reasoning there !

who dreams her
who raises beyond her history
the curtains of fire
& cypress tree & the olive tree
& the tree of grace ?

whose face must she dream / whose dream must she face ?

we walk without moving through the trance
& the green; silent & sated & moist & serene

at odds with the dreamer but at one with the dream
beyond time; beyond logic; beyond ART & desire

to where my eyes meet her eyes
& they blaze they blaze in a dream's dark fire

th lesson

it ws the attic messenger
came to me in a dream

& all abt
his sirens were

as white birds
on th green

& in his hand
there sprang a heart

to tell what i
must say

& from that heart
there blew a rose

th low winds bore
away

& on each petal
of that rose

th slow worm lay
soft curl'd

& in th book
of this quiet fire

i read
what delphi told

th passing &
th passing &

the passing of
a world.

7. Poetry Live !

always merrie & bright

(blues for henry miller, 9.6.80)

no more beaujolais
no more strumpet
no more croissants
no more crumpet
no more gauloise blue
no /
      nor erik satie trumpet

& no more squirt henry
& a chunda ! hen & ah
do be
do be

do . . .

well
i read the katzenjammer kids
before i ever read you
& marvelled at this genesis
yr art laid on like glew
thinkin'
             / how come

how come ! th flatus
all divine
eludes you in th blue
while all abt /
         th high
domed bards
ws anglin' at th true ?

wooah!

it ws th marriage
of heaven & hell
y wanted as yr due

wit yr squirt, henry
& y chunda !
yeah.
& y do be
doo bee
do

truth is hen
we loved ya best when
you ws werst /
                              didn't know
what t'do.
yeah. human
ALL TOO HUMAN
henry
& human through
& through
                              /...

well now,

no more pernod
& no more whores
& no more publishers
& no more wars
& no more enlightened souls
to use you for their cause

                              /...

yeah.

221

where books are read
before they're burned
we will remember you

wit yor sqert
henry
& y chunder !

& yr do be do be do be do be
    do be do be do

ahem,

well now,
down heah in
little old green
new zealand
in mount eden at
20 minutes after 5
        dah da dah
dah   Daaaaaaaaaaa

i learn on lookin' at
the evening star you
are
no more alive . . . ! . . . merde !

        hot dawg !

        haaand jive !

better than runyon
better than thurber
better than nash
yeah. 'n' better than
boris karloff too &
better than johnny cash

better than mccullers &
mcclure & mckuen
who sell more books
than jesus does
cs they know jes what
they're doin . . .

better than doris day
johnny ray
& good , good golly
miss molly
better in time , almost
i guess . . .
almost better 'n buddy
holly !

yeah.

better 'n a tonic better 'n
home brew
& better 'n nine
tenths th heads
        / that poured the
        acid
        on yew . . .

yeah. where books
are READ before
they're burned
        we'll remember you

wit yor squoit
hen
& jaw thunder

& j do be do be
   do be do be
   do be do be
      do . . .

well now,
let me jes say down here
at length
before this ever lovin'
little old wank is thru !

there's still a voice
in the midnight choir
turns a crack'd lament
for you

yeah

better than yevtushenko & bicycles
(but not as good as Babi Yar)
better than harry
better than truman
yeah. & capote . . .
better than warhol & don juan b far
& quezacotl
& peyote . . .

& better 'n most of th beatniks, too
henry

with your squirt
and your chunder
and your

do be do be
do be do be
do be do be
   do . . .

well now,
I knows y hankered on th muse !
yet
ch did not deride her
&
we will not heah one
snide remark
no !
nor moreso corso snyder

yeah

& while i close
this evening star
eat
kerouac cold spaghetti
no charmaine greer
nor ginsberg tear
cd make me ferlinghetti

where books are read
before they're burned
we will remember yew !

wit yr squirt , henry
& yr chunda , henry &

yr do
  be

  do
  be

  do
  be

do be
do / be doo bee doo.

reflexions on a gift
of guava jelly

m wee neighbour
in mt eden

always folds her arms
when she walks

up belle vue road
t m gate

like she's continually
tuckin' hersel' in

y'ken . . .

one squally tuesday
she produced a jar

of jam

a comfiture from th noble
guava

& waived her receipt
of my thanks

with a sturdy
' not at a'
  not at a' '

it ws pleasant
i had it on toast

wi m'afternoon tea.

occasionally
she appears at th rock wall

hr silver hair above the scoria
hr blue eye sharp as a sparrow's

behind her woolworth's specs
that make do wi' one lug

& we converse.

there are many, many very
interesting & curious things

have occurred in her time
& in her garden . . .

truth t'tell . . .

                    / well

she's an auld dear
as you can no doubt see . . .

but what wd she accept as a gift
from me ?

sometimes i feel like giving her a hug
but its nae proper . . . ! / besides

her mon / her mon—he's 83 !
her mon's in th privy

or the leekbed &
there's naught he doesna see !

och. we'el
och. we'el

we converse / but
what can i gie her

frae m'ain plot
seeded parsley?

blighted spuds ?
bland, middle aged garlick ?

och we'el
we converse

as th year settles
& turns . . .

cn she / cd she know
that i'm one o' they

madcap poets
a few years older

than rabbie burns ?

t'be sure , i'll think
o' something . . .

as we converse
as we converse

/ its nae use
  its nae use . . . och

we'el wee mither
wd y'accept

yon serious
verse ?

its uncou' real
d'y'ken

john peel
d'y'ken

the apple
& pear

marketing board . . .

och. we'el
this poem's a wee

dock fr doris / fr
auld lang syne

frae glascie
fr th turning

o' th wheel !

this poem's
a wee bouquet

fr culloden
fr gretna green
fr th new age
m'dear
—th like o' which
we've never seen . . .

here's tae
th far coulins
here's tae
the hippocrene !

och we'el
auld neighbour

here's tae our
conceit

o' th butcher'd
nazarene ! aye

daily seen . . .

here's tae
auld reekie !

auld lang syne
aye

& greenoch
& gouroch

aye . & skye &
aberdeen.

la condition humaine
(man's estate)

here's yellow dandelions on clover
beyond hydrangeas green with sap
& unbloom'd yet
before my back porch step
here's white butterflies
in waltzing pairs
along the hedgerow & through
a bamboo thicket
here's daisies white & gold
beneath an olive sill
& clouds like winsome lambs
reflected in this glass
of prussian blue
here's flax, luxuriant, simple
on the greensward
forget me nots against a lichen'd fence
& russet hues of starlings wings & thrushes
& sparrows throats & heads
as busy on the green of afternoon
as on the blue
busy on the green these late summer hours
the long afternoon through

here's pine & macrocarpa & the peach tree
majestic with the lazy drone
of bees
& apple branches weighted like a father's arms
at yule
& plums that ripen quietly
in the dappled shade

here's choko tendrils bent on scoria walls
& snails & ants among the ginger weed
here's balance & possession & economy
here's order joy & whimsy
& no greed

here's adolescent sunflower slender sturdy
here's aged bamboo clumps as good as gone
here's harmony & logic & enchantment
here's algebra & opera & plainsong

here's lava flow & fumarole & basalt
here's wasp & blowfly; mosquitos in the windbreak
here's corrugated iron & weatherboard
here's arachne & long fang'd rat but yet no snake

so let us sing together for mount eden
its borough hall its village & its gaol
& let us praise the wisemen & the systems
that do & do & do for us all & will not fail

& let us now & then down to the oval
to see the sacred cricket & rugby there
& let us boo the ragged demonstrators
who spoil the sport of white men everywhere

& who would not live long here in mount eden
& close his heart & mind & balls & face
praise god; the baptist church & television
& protect our real estate ; this lovely place.

street of early sorrows
ship of 50s fooles

(a drinking song)

do you have a street in mind
anna
one that comes down on you
from behind a low hill
foreigners wd call
a mountain . . .

a way that wends its weight
through time's cold maze
to break, illuminated

into the sudden sun
of memory
or
a harbour like a dream
like a find !
pure castilian fountain
protected by 10,000 pines
anna
do you have a street in mind ?

as tranced travellers from
another star
might feel on waking to that first
strong hint of solar flare
against iron pluto

against familiar indigo

& fixing then their sights
on this green pretty globe
rejoice

233

beyond all science to find
we are

as they
are . . .

2 parts water 1 part rock
& 3 parts desire . . .

do you have a ship in mind
anna
the dark barge we did not know
but recognised

in 1957

poled westwards by the faceless shades
who toiled, it seemed, for every purpose
under heaven
against literature & education & psychology
while we stood, musing, losing
for a moment !
the strictures of these things . . .
in the wellington mist
on the kelburn viaduct
below the tinakori hills
in heartbreak hotel . . .

where the barmaid's fat
canary sat

singing as a caged bird sings
in frigid trills

' twhoo whoo whoo whooit '
just like that

trimm'd wings but noble
& fey & puzzled & pluck't

& pecking, pecking
on the little swinging
swinging
ringing bell. everybody dressed in black
& waterfront blues
while you flew off above it all
now ain't that news

& y never did come back . . .
knowing full well
you were leaving me the hard ship
the steward ship
of kiwi duty &
of booze. now if you shd chance
upon this rort !
don't be surprised at what y find
but tell me , tell me
my sometime golden friend

on time's sad swell
o truth to tell

did ya evah have a ship in mind ?

ah . . . baby blue
it ws you / it ws you !

on the yacht marina
at oriental bay

divining ancient craft
as they passed by

inchoate to th werlde
as poetry !

but blode heat warm as honey
in our teenage mouths

aching with surfeit &
largesse

of love. first love   &
nineteen-fifties   ah

tenderness . . .

beneath the pt jerningham cannon
its fell retort

beneath the dismal foghorns
homeboats 50s sounds

in that up tight seaport
beneath the dogs & hounds

of the mazengarb report

beneath the glockenspiel
carillon

in the night /
beyond

the convent on
the hill

that brought tears & smiles
for vespers then

that brings them still . . .

tell me , darling, on time's
deep

bell. on truth's full swell
did you ever have a ship in mind ?

& if you perhaps, lover
have in mind an inn

an evening out
in northern hills

an acquiescence then
to time & beauty

still
beyond us both

yet one, one
anna

do you have , in mind
an inn ?

then drink lover ! should
you chance

this idiot raft
on this white page

gliding past
some hard bleak

thoroughfare of years
—yr gallic middle age . . .

drink lover ! to yr salted
sundered venice

to yr young , yr promised
poet

in antipodean backwash now
& painted , here , gondola
black

all for yr drown'd
yr perished souvenirs . . .

drink lover ! fr every chime
& bell

along the valleys of th rhone
& loire / drink ! fr artaud !

fr st lazare !
for ' bonjour tristesse '

sunset on the foreshore &
moonrise on the cable car

for our drunken boat
that we sailed so well

sober as virgins
grave as true friends . . .

drink for our desert wars
to make amends

drink fr ben jonson
fr th song that never ends

drink to old karori road
its '38 V8 twists

& its bends . . .

drink to the hutt river
valley juvenile delinquents

some we numbered as friends

ah . . . drink anna !   drink
to the student prince

& to young, buddy holly
never seen since !

drink deep on nothin !
every chime, mignon,
every bell

fr th thirst , fr th desert
fr ' too much , too much a

nothin ! '

for your rock 'n' roll
finesse

ah ! legendary—
for hydromel . . .

drink lover ! & you were
a pretty mother baby &

you knew it quite well !
when kelburn ws all over pink

roses & y'made aro street
look just like that as well

when wellington for a matter of months
resembled paradise. yeah. & paris

resembled hell . . .

once, before we met
—off some island

in a full rigg'd naval whaler
i had seen it quite well

you were to be my constant , nemesis
for what werdes could not tell

it was t'be some kind of vision
like chagall's / like mccahon's

rachmaninov trimmed th canvas
botticelli sang softly

& i told the yarns . . .

primavera, primavera
i ws a countin' on you . . .

et tu, penelope , et tu ?
& the myths
& the sagas

are they still coming true ?

anna
our parents died quietly
as parents often do

anna
our children are grown now
yet still i think of you

our youthful dreams
have been tortured by
degrees , by degrees
& our ships list
a few
tell me, are we still
sounding vessels
for love's swete first dream
that keeps coming through ?

or is it youth's wines
the tart cup on its lees
on its lees
baby blue baby blue
&
are we yet vikings to nowhere
from the sounds of the true ?

as you were. as you do
beginning & end
but tell me, my sometime
golden friend . . .

did you ever have a harbour
like a dream like a find !
like a street like an inn;
anna did you ever have
a ship in mind ?

Armageddon / Hokitika Blue

Well, I sat down by the Bluespur mine
down West Coast—Hokitika way
& I sat & I watched the gorse bushes grow
in the high clear bloom of the day

& I watched the free gulls & the wee sparrows too
over township & scrub bush & sand
& I thought of the past & I thought of the now
& the future the good Lord has planned

& I noted the weatherboard houses set there
each harbouring a filled washing line
& a myriad pale colours against the blue sky
hung there in clear weather & fine

yeah, hundreds of work shirts strung in the gold sun
red, pink, mauve, yellow and green
yet y'know as I went through that quiet little town
no white collar there could be seen

& in the main street there stood a clock tower
first unveil'd in 1903
& on the reverse a white tablet of names
writ large for eternity

Victoria's legacy; a kind of a heaven
hers & Albert's too, I suppose
but another Royal—Edward, No. 7—
was mentioned—or George—one of those

& I looked at the clock & the houses & lawns
& the washing hung out there so clean
at the squat working trousers & faded work shirts
& the stiff woollen socks in between

& I thought of the glacier land I'd come through
& the blue lipp'd crevasses I'd seen
& I thought of the miners blue lipp'd at God's gate
& the diggers red eyed on God's green

of the Scots at Culloden; of the Irish Cromwell
of the Holy Lands / Holy Crusaders there too
& I thought of this heritage the truth for to tell
of the ordinary folks & the true

of Balaclava, Bloemfontein, Passchendaele, Flanders Fair
of Gallipoli, Cassino, yes, Dunkirk too
& I thought of Nagasaki & Hiroshima there
& Mai Lai, Viet Nam; well—wouldn't you ?

& I thought of those men who go down in the ground
for blue coal; & the brown & the black
& I thought of the workmanlike soldier boys , too
—West Coasters: who never came back

Then I stood there, Ginna, in the afternoon gold
pond'ring yellowcake , arms race insanity
deep sad thoughts , love, as blue as the coal
of a future for you and for me

& I thought of this wandering , poet's trade that I chose
& of the scholars that politick there
& marvell'd how seldom the poet's revealed
in ordinary working people everywhere

& I wondered , as no doubt, many have before
why innocence seems born just to die
open form, open seam, open field, open dream
open wounds gaping under the sky

so I dumbly rose up & took up my pen
to make a formal poem for you
to mine in the rock of life for love's warmth
like the diggers of old used to do

for if it should come & come to the worst
I would fight to protect what I love
—still, discourse & tolerance , is my maverick hope
my sole prayer to the Royal up above

Then along Sewell Street I took me a walk
past the redbrick Department of Lands
Lo ! —high on a stone framed by Tasman & Cook
King Dick Richard John Seddon he stands

& in his right hand he holds a white scroll
—what's on it I could not quite tell—
but he was a white man & in his white time
knew white paradise & white hell

still, I thought of the Maori landgrab he allow'd
this country's still trying to fix
& of that nadir of Maori population so proud
in Eighteen Hundred and Ninety-six

Then I considered our Govt our Church & our State
& the slit eyed peacocks that legislate there
& rejoiced in the wallet of my heart for their great
—grave concern ! —fan flaunted everywhere

& I passed by the grey concrete, green tiled & fair
all Saints true blue angels church hall
& I watched by the square , bowman's tower set up there
the irregular autumn leaves fall

—then, sat I down blue, by the Bluespur mine
down West Coast—Hokitika way
& I sighed as I watched the early stars shine
at the sharp , clear end of the day

& I watched the ducks with their young ones go
down a creek over brown & white sand
& I thought of the past & I thought of the now
& the future the good Lord has planned.

ANZAC DAY, 1983

CODA

poets to come

on hampstead heath
on hampstead heath

twelve years
after
first standing
in that green
magnificence

twelve years
of rutted
goat tracks
on
    the
        serpentine
           ridge

of
what will come
to be known
as the saddest
hardest
decade of the century

twelve years
of the scotch
& th bourbons
& th huguenots

& fire
      & water
under the bridge

i amuse myself
finding exact
locations

of former
good times
amours—

time trips !

stoned
unguided tours

th sun still looks like
blake's baby face
to me

the green / th green
star

' something the size of a guinea '

that presages th host
singing holy holy holy . . .

yeah.   th sky above &
            the earth beneath
            on hampstead heath
            on hampstead heath . . .

there
in the dales / & vales
gainsborough is snoring
& hogarth & turner
& pale cockney johnny / albion's seed /
waiting to be born / hark !

what is this late sound breaking
on the ear ?

th city bells
from far
off

chime

& th village bells from near

it is th dead centre
of th year

midsummer's eve—

&
i am stricken
slowly

if such a thing might be
thinking of the great
unborn

who are not here

leaning on th bells
that break

on every ear

looking on th heath
& sky

pondering those novel
bards

who were

& did

but are not here /   waiting to be born
                      hark ! as on th cool
                      romantic glow
                      of sunset
                                now
                                        i hear

the sanskrit tongue of bagpipes &
                      the haunted gold
                      of one
                                french horn . . .

here's to th green ; the unborn !
th poets are coming !
(like always)

here's to th green ! here's to th year !
th poets are coming ! They're almost here !

Note on the text

IN DECEMBER 1999, WITH THE HELP of his daughter Genevieve, David Mitchell photocopied those of his poems that he had to hand and wished to preserve; it took the best part of a week. The collected poems make up three thick, bound, blue-covered A4 books of photocopies that include many lists and notations. Book I, the slimmest of the three, collects the poems from 1957 to 1969; Book II, which is thicker, covers 1970 to 1979; and Book III, thickest of all, goes from 1980 to 1994; altogether they include (depending on how the count is made) some three hundred poems.

Mitchell brought these Blue Books with him to Sydney in March 2006. It is from them that we have made the selection here: about one quarter of those available, largely from Books I and II but with some of the longer poems from Book III included. In doing so we have taken as our guide Mitchell's own choice of which version he wished to photocopy: the typescripts include multiple versions of many of the poems. The versions from the Blue Books have been checked against any published version and also with typescript versions; most variations are minor and where choices had to be made, we have usually preferred to follow published versions over those in the Blue Books; and those in the Blue Books over typescript versions.

A related concern was how to lay the poems out on the page. Some texts are clearly scored for performance; others seem cramped on the page, as if paper were at a premium. Again, where a poem has been previously printed we have used that as a guide; for the unpublished poems we have tried to reproduce Mitchell's own spacing; and where doubt exists have applied the principle that the words need plenty of room: white paper against which they can be distinctly seen, a silence against which they can be distinctly heard. *Pipe Dreams in Ponsonby* has been our template here.

There are two poems—'at dusk' and 'melba hooks'—for which no manuscript text was found; their original layout is unknown and the versions here have been transcribed from sound recordings. We have Mitchell's consent to include these poems. It is very likely that there are other poems, not yet come to light, that survive only as sound recordings. 'A small sincere poem for Davnet' was published in *Free Poetry* (Sydney) in 1970 and evidently Mitchell retained no copy of it; it is not in the Blue Books. Nor is 'Dark Fire', which exists only as a typescript as revised in 1980. There are no typescripts of the twenty-six poems in *Pipe Dreams in Ponsonby* that were written in 1971; they are represented in the Blue Books as photocopies of pages of the book as published by Stephen Chan.

The order of this selection generally follows that of the Blue Blooks, which are chronological to the extent of arranging the poems of *Pipe Dreams in Ponsonby* in their order of composition rather than as they appear in the book; but we have departed from this order in three cases. The sequence 'lemon tree' / 'night through the orange window' / 'Forty Words on Three 'where's' is placed at the beginning of section three rather than where Mitchell has the poems, just after 'VERY FLAT HORIZONS !' and before 'slow trip above atlantis'. This was done to maintain a sense of a narrative throughout section two; and because the sequence has strong affinities with the other poems in section three. 'yellow room', which was written in Sydney in 1966, instead of sitting with 'harlequin' in *Pipe Dreams in Ponsonby* or amongst the other poems in section three with which it is contemporary, now introduces 'Myths of Woolloomooloo'; and 'poets to come' provides a coda—it dates from 1975 but was re-written in 1980 for performance during the State of the Nation tour.

Where, in the Blue Books, there are two versions of the same poem we have usually chosen the later one; most rewrites seem to have been for the purpose of an upcoming performance. We have omitted the sonnets; there are only six or seven of these, three in Book I and three (or four) in Book III, and they are consciously antique if not antiquated, and sit awkwardly amongst the rest of the work. With the exception of 'Armageddon / Hokitika Blue', we haven't selected from the ballads, of which there are quite a few long ones, thinking that they might merit a volume of their own. Nor have we included any other of the 'Poems for Ginna'; the sequence is better read entire.

Finally, a word on punctuation. Mitchell's was both eccentric and inconsistent and we have decided against standardising his more obvious innovations—he sometimes, not always, puts a space before as well as after a comma; or a space before an exclamation mark, a question mark, a full stop. He also inserted extra spaces within parentheses and after and before quotation marks. We have followed him in these particulars; and in his variable use of capitals and lower case in titles and within poems. However, we have departed from his manuscripts in one particular, inserting a narrow space both before and after the forward slash wherever it appears. It's worth remembering that all Mitchell poems benefit from being read out loud and that his textual innovations were always made as guides towards performance of the poem.

Acknowledgements

The editors would like to express their thanks to Ross Mitchell, Ann Edwards, Sara Mitchell and Genevieve McClean for the access they allowed to the Mitchell family papers.

Particular acknowledgement is due to Paul Gray for being an unstinting and tireless guide to Mitchell's life and oeuvre. To Gill Ward, who found the lost and the unlocatable. And to Elsebeth Nielson, the sine qua non.

We are also indebted to the following: Graham Baigent, Eric Beach, Norman Bilbrough, Maureen Birchfield, Kevin Boon, Roger Brittenden, Tom Carment, Stephen Chan, Alan Daylight, Murray Edmond, Peter Frater, Marti Friedlander, Tom Finlayson, Bill Gruar, Batch Hales, Russell Haley, Donald Kerr, Francis Kuipers, Michele Leggott, Barry Lett, Alan Loney, Alison McClean, Graham McGregor, June McMillan, Chris Moisa, Mike Morrisey, Ian Mune, Gary Mutton, Keith Nicolson, Peter Olds, Stephen Oliver, John Parkyn, Alistair Paterson, Mark Pirie, Trevor Reeves, Ron Riddell, Jan Kemp Riemenschneider, Ian Rockel, the late Martyn Sanderson, Michael Sharkey, Iain Sharp, Barry Southam, David Tossman, Denys Trussell, Ian Wedde, Paul Wotherspoon and Mark Young.

Index of titles and first lines

*Poem titles are in **bold**.*